I0752888

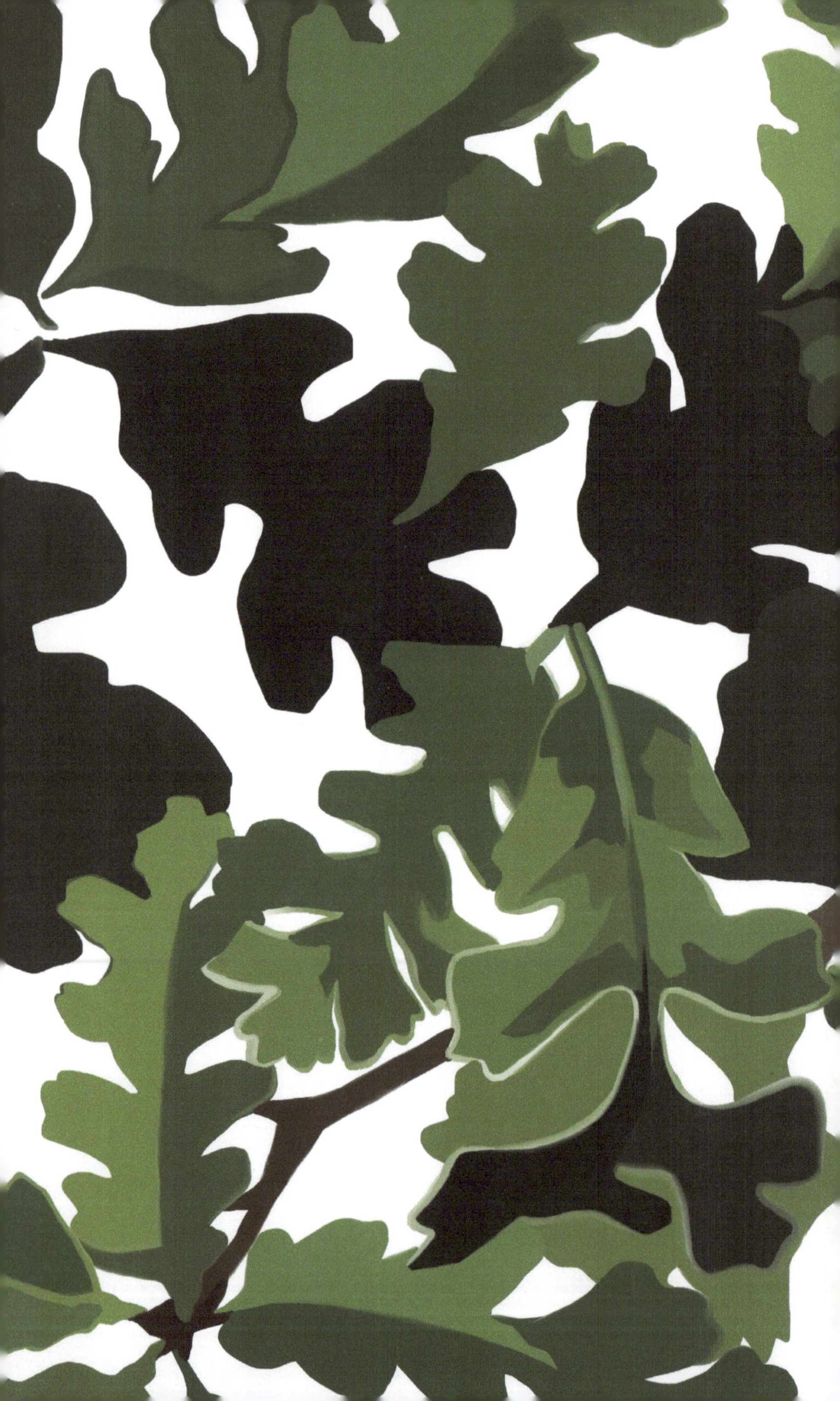

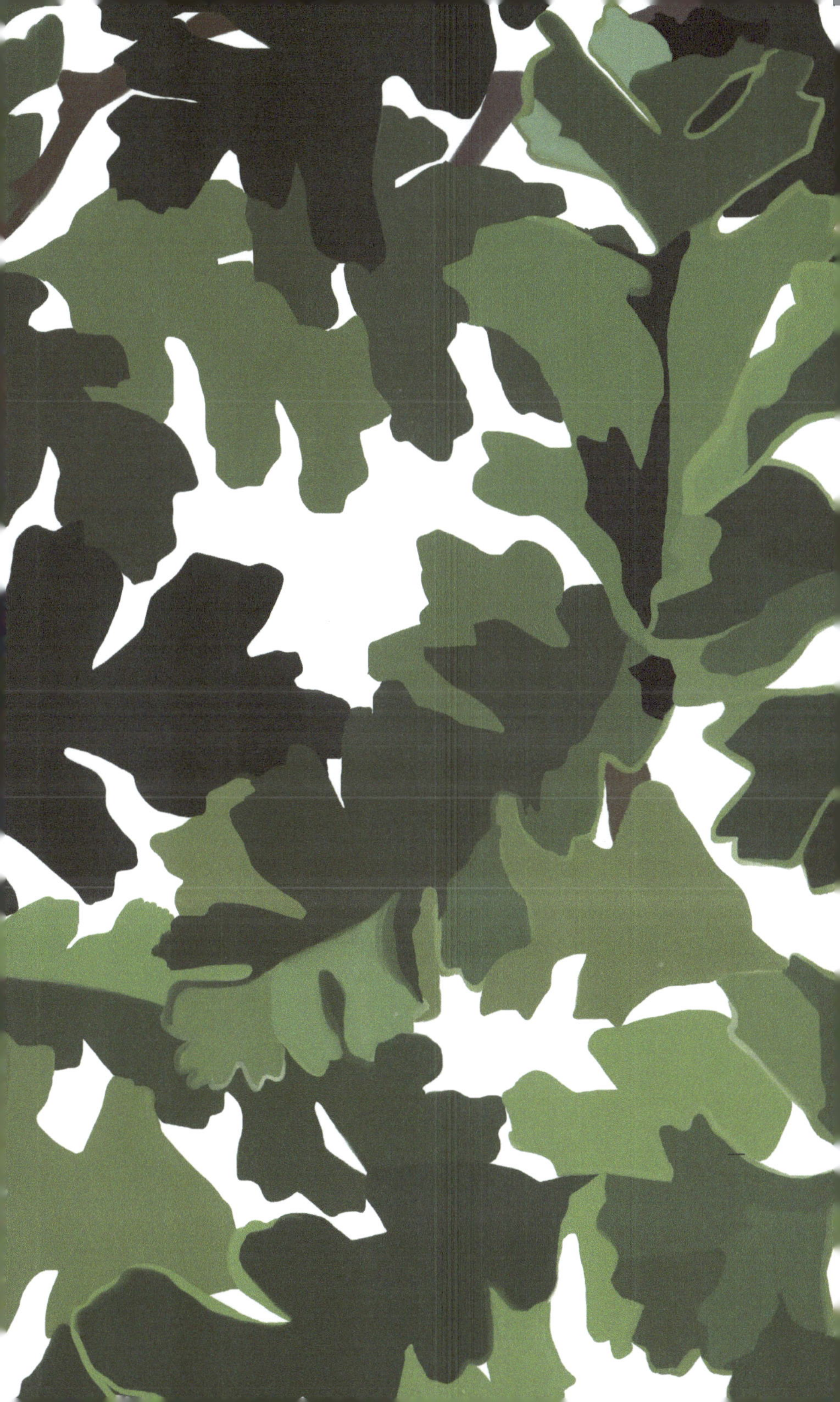

ASIAN

a nature walk guide by

AMERICAN

Chopsticks Alley Art

HEALING

Poetry • Art • Meditation

Cover illustration by Roan Victor
Cover design by Cynthia Cao

First Edition
Published by Chopsticks Alley Art

Chopsticks Alley Art
ChopsticksAlleyArt.org
ChopsticksAlley.com

Mailing Address:
88 S 3rd Street #183
San Jose, CA 95113
Email: ChopsticksAlley@gmail.com

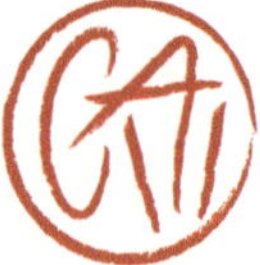

You can search throughout the entire universe
for someone who is more deserving of your love
and affection than you are yourself,
and that person is not to be found anywhere.

You yourself, as much as anybody in the entire
universe deserves your love and affection.

– Buddha

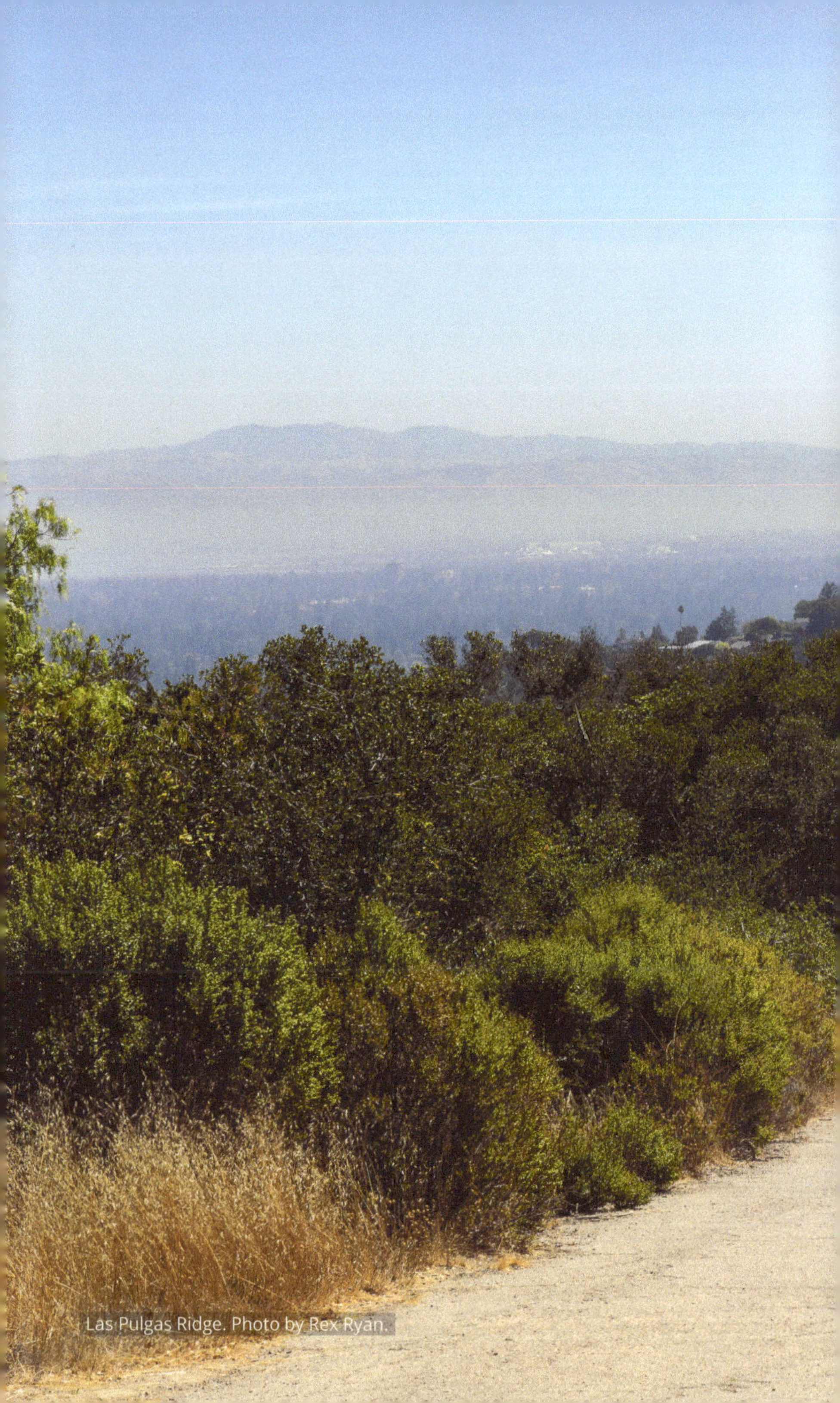

Las Pulgas Ridge. Photo by Rex Ryan.

CONTENTS

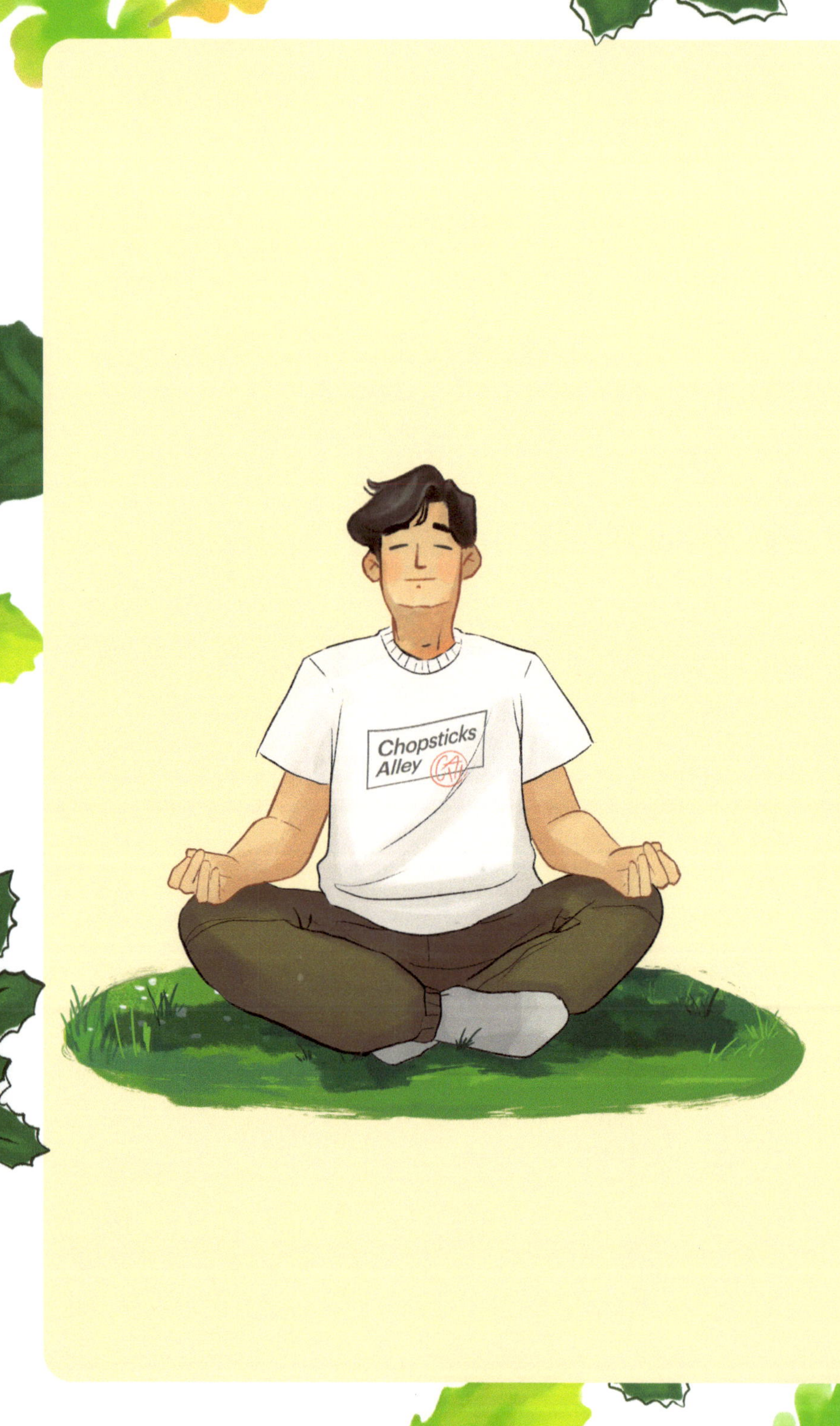
Chopsticks
Alley

Introduction

In writing this *Asian American Healing (AAH) Nature Walk Guide*, Chopsticks Alley Art is sharing with you a glimpse of Asian art, culture, philosophy, and the relationship our communities have with nature.

With the help of our partner, Peninsula Open Space Trust (POST), we have collected a list of recommended parks that you may leisurely explore. The intent is to share new ways to experience nature, encouraging you to enjoy our local parks more, express your creativity, and improve your mental health.

The *AAH Nature Walk Guide* will help you *Release* daily stress, *Reconnect* with yourself and others, and *Reclaim* your source of joy.

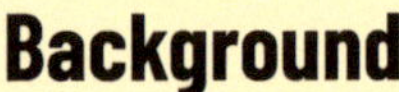

Background

The Santa Clara County Health Officer issued an order for individuals living in the county to shelter in place on March 16, 2020. We could only leave our homes to receive services or perform essential work. All indoor businesses and places were closed. Public gatherings were prohibited to avoid the spread of the deadly Coronavirus.

Thankfully, local and state parks remained open, and during these past three years, public parks have seen a surge in visitors as more people have sought ways to get outdoors safely. As you fall in love with the outdoors, we hope you will also become good stewards of these spaces.

Meditations

Chopsticks Alley Art created a weekly streaming program titled Medi-Veggie, where we offered short meditations, featured artists' artworks and stories, and shared vegetarian recipes to help viewers manage the stress the pandemic created. We started incorporating short meditations from this program in our meetings, programming, and art classes too!

This practice is now commonplace at Chopsticks Alley. Short meditations are not intimidating or difficult for beginners to follow. This practice is a valuable tool to help manage stress, anxiety, and life's challenges.

Mental Health

Self-care is NOT selfish: it is time for our community to accept how critical it is for our mental health to receive priority.

Together, we can work to increase awareness and support to end the stigma surrounding mental health among the Asian community.

These three pillars play a major role in upholding mental health:

- **Belonging**
  A community can provide a sense of belonging where you feel safe, seen, heard, and understood.

- **Support**
  It helps to have someone to share your challenges and joys.

- **Purpose**
  Although you may not be aware of this, you bring meaning to other people through the various roles you play in their lives. Being of service to others will help you feel important, and it is also rewarding to know you can help uplift others.

Take the time to reflect, build, and connect with like-minded people. Healthy relationships should make you feel safe and comfortable.

Meet An Thạnh

He first appeared as the Boat Guide in Chopsticks Alley Art's book *ARTventure Down the Mekong*, and has since adopted Joey from AARF.

An Thạnh and his loyal companion Joey will be your Nature Guides throughout this book. Together, they will take you on a healing journey with nature.

Get your walking shoes, water bottles, snacks, leash, and bags ready!

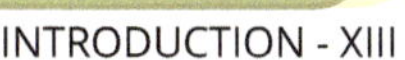

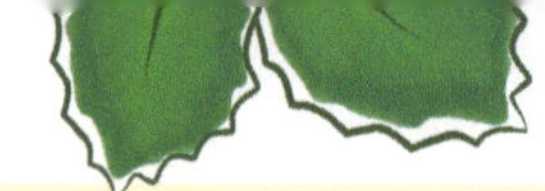

The *AAH Nature Walk Guide* is organized into these categories, but may be used in any order you wish. You will see these symbols throughout the guide:

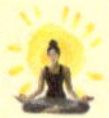 Meditation recommendations

 Recommendations to local parks

 Dog-friendly parks

 Suggested creative activities and prompts

 Self-care tips

Share this *AAH Nature Walk Guide* with others. *Better yet, ask them to join you on your walks!*

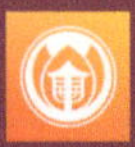 **Meditation App** 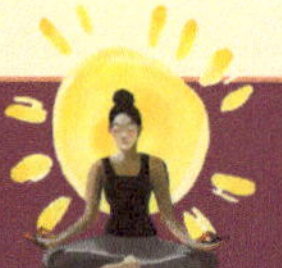

There are many meditation apps you can take with you on your walks. Chopsticks Alley recommends **Plum Village** app because it is free and offers a wide variety of meditations created by the AAPI community. Meditations are in multiple languages and can be downloaded in advance. We have received permission to share the app with you.

Tip: Download the Plum Village app and each meditation before you leave the house so you can access them in areas without cell signals.

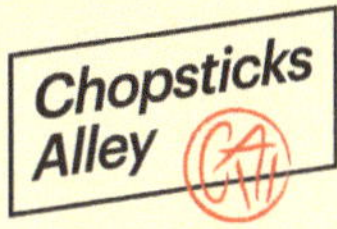

About Chopsticks Alley Art

Chopsticks Alley promotes Southeast Asian cultural heritage through the arts. It celebrates the cultural diversity of Southeast Asian contemporary art to foster greater understanding and connect communities.

Chopsticks Alley offers arts-based programs and classes, exhibits, and community events to create an engaging environment of celebration, understanding, and support among diverse, multi-generational communities.

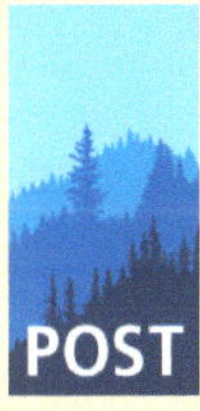

About Peninsula Open Space Trust

POST protects open space on the Peninsula and in the South Bay for the benefit of all.

POST is creating a network of protected lands where people and nature can connect and thrive. These lands are preserved forever so present and future generations benefit from the careful balance of rural and urban landscapes that make our region extraordinary.

Since its founding in 1977, POST has preserved over 86,000 acres of open space in San Mateo, Santa Clara, and Santa Cruz counties. These protected lands include permanent open spaces, farms, and parks.

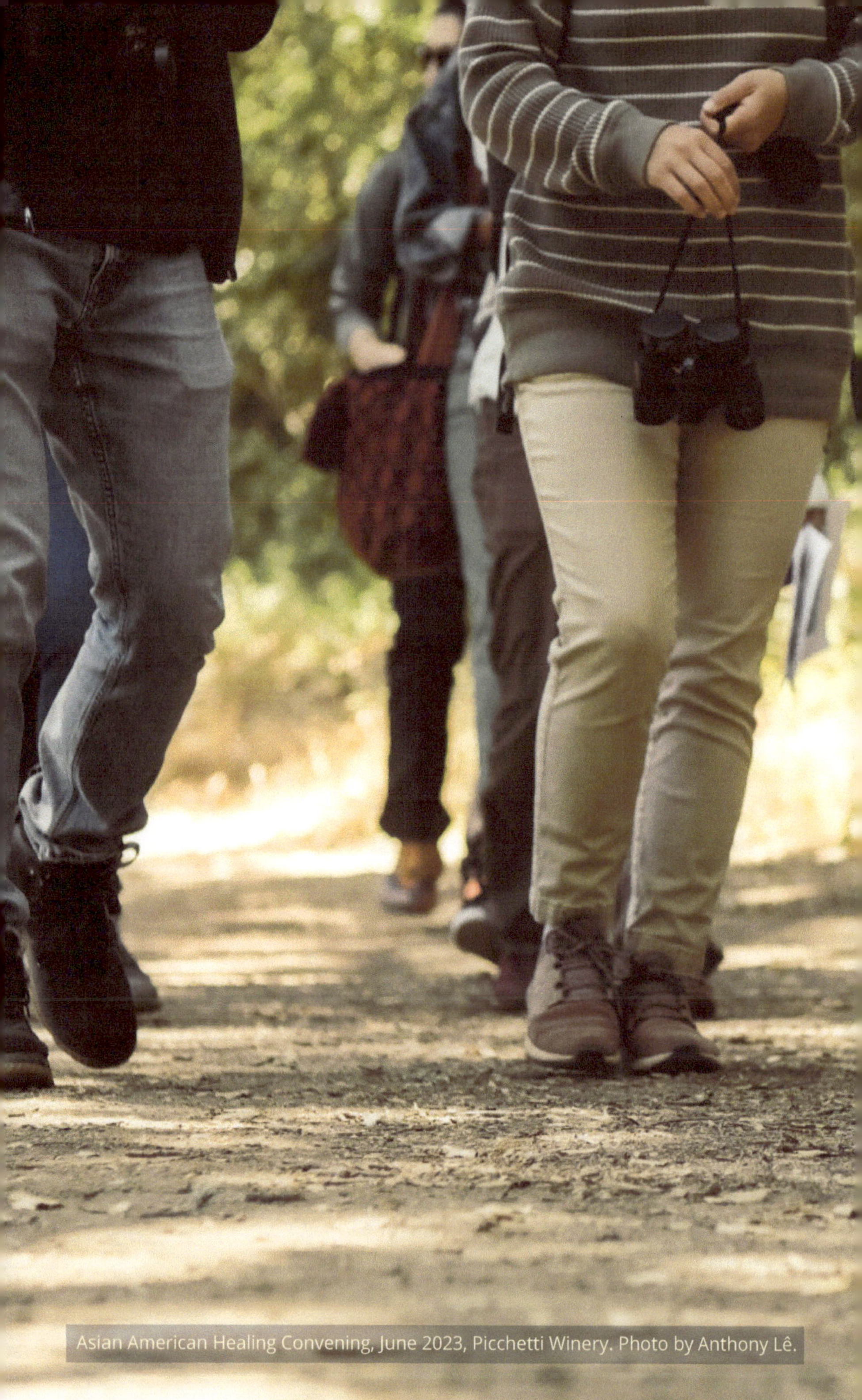

Asian American Healing Convening, June 2023, Picchetti Winery. Photo by Anthony Lê.

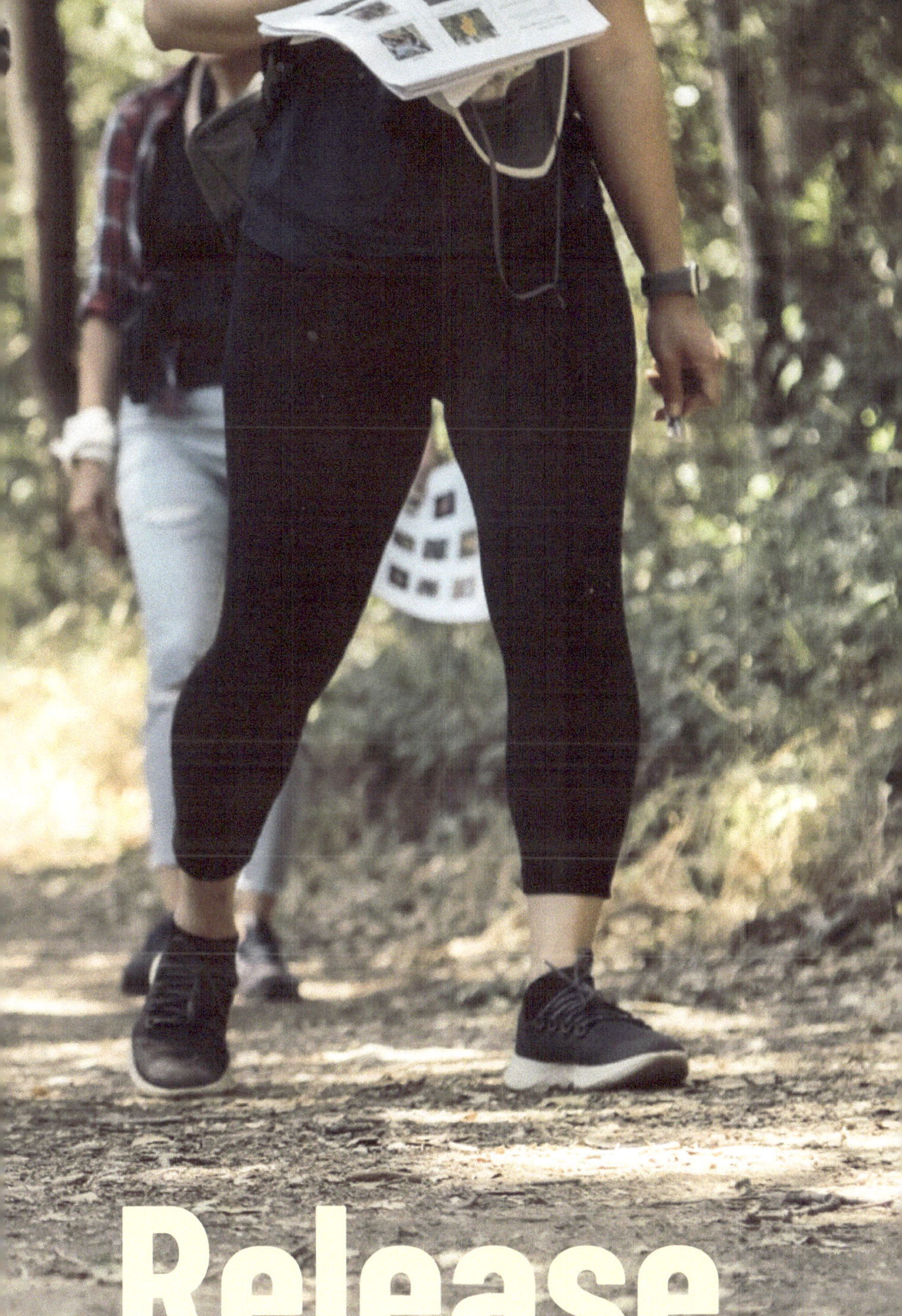

Release

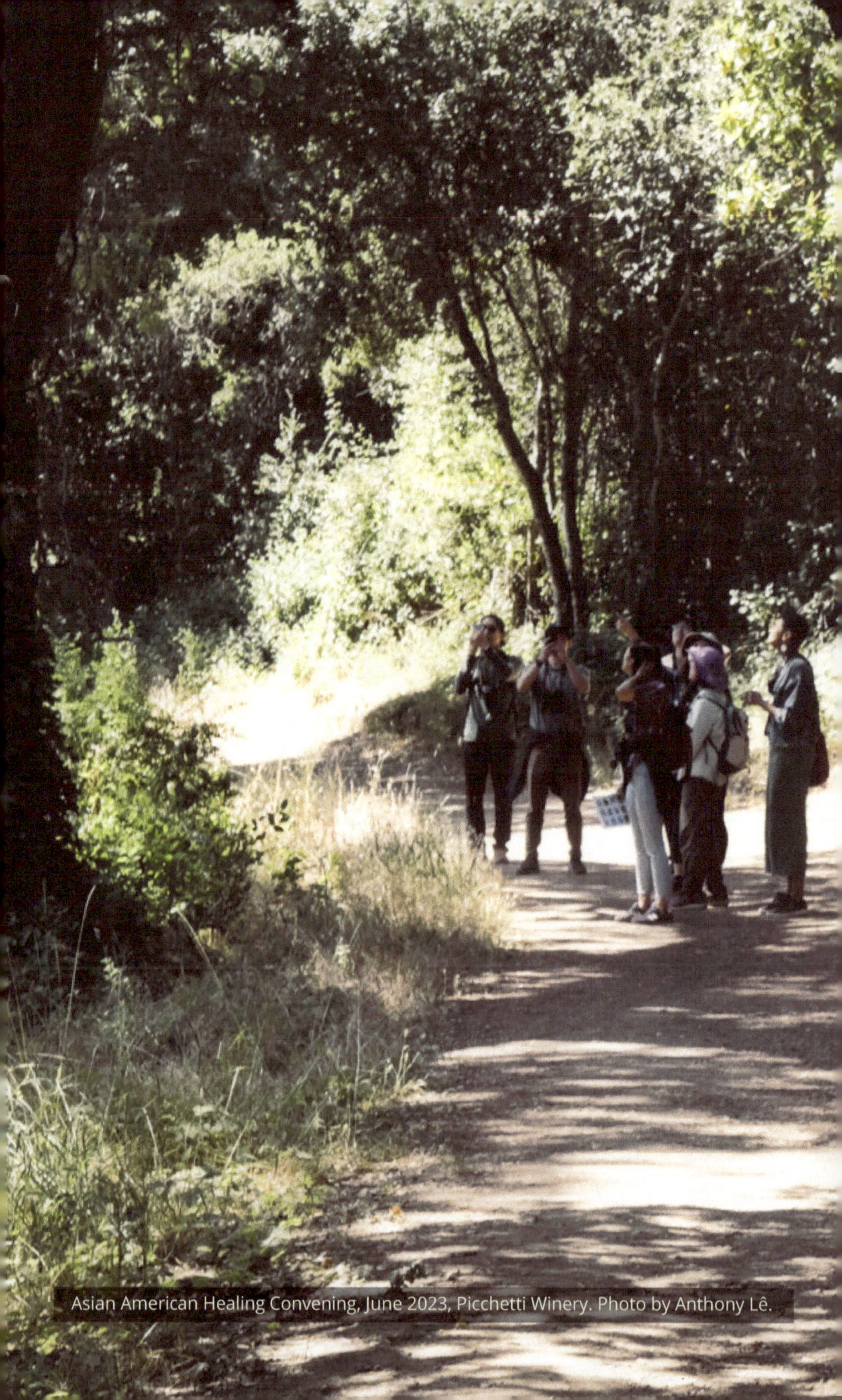
Asian American Healing Convening, June 2023, Picchetti Winery. Photo by Anthony Lê.

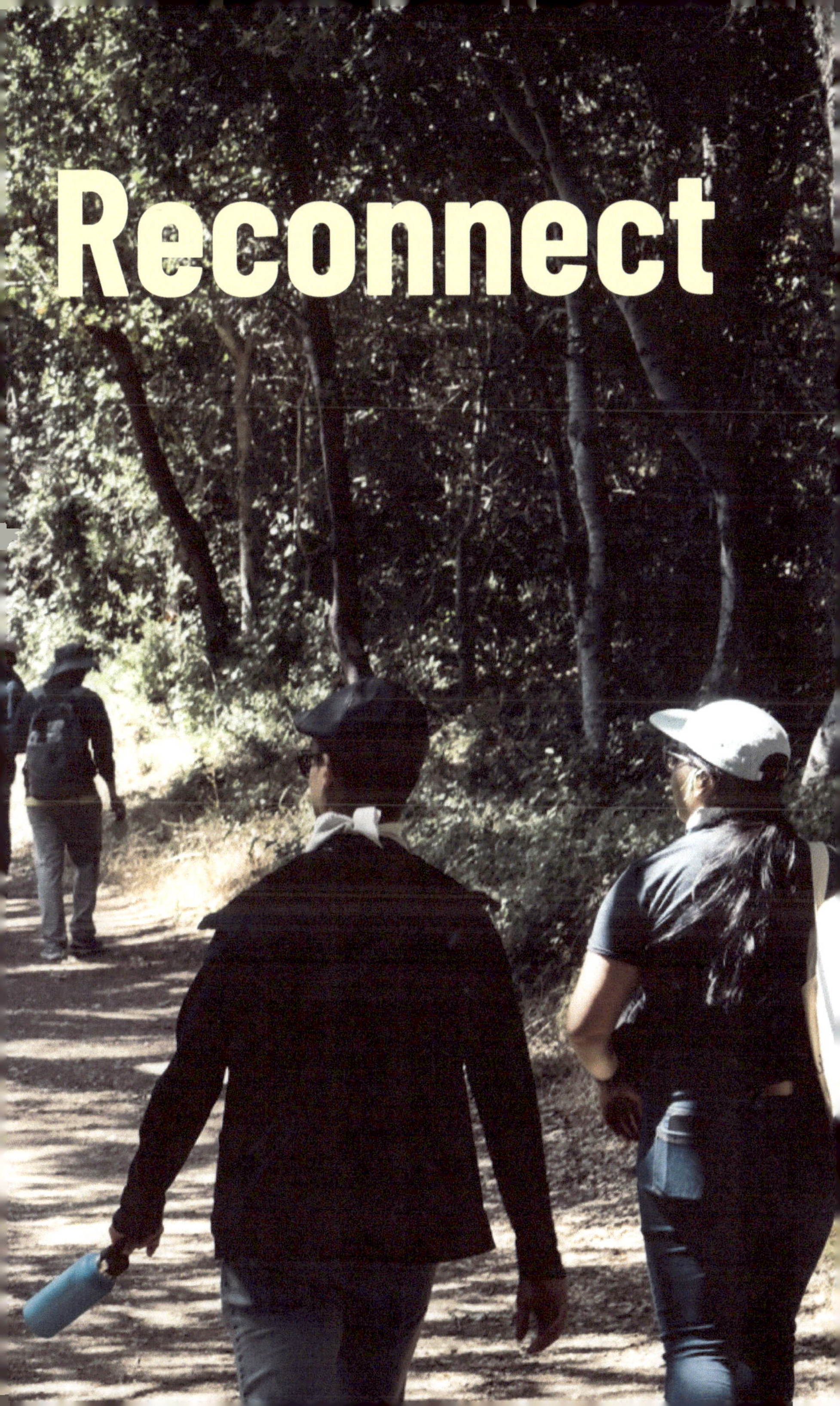
Reconnect

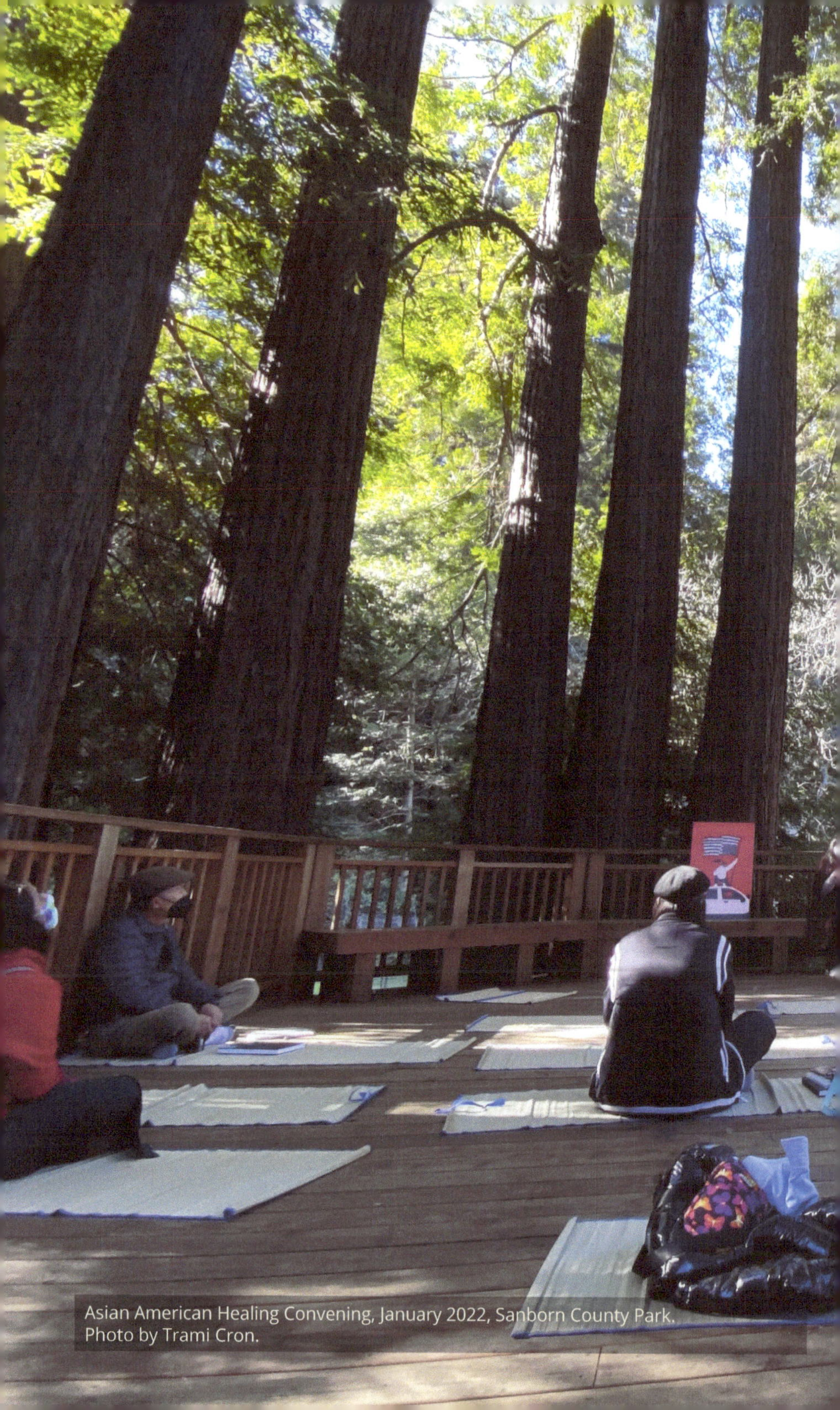

Asian American Healing Convening, January 2022, Sanborn County Park.
Photo by Trami Cron.

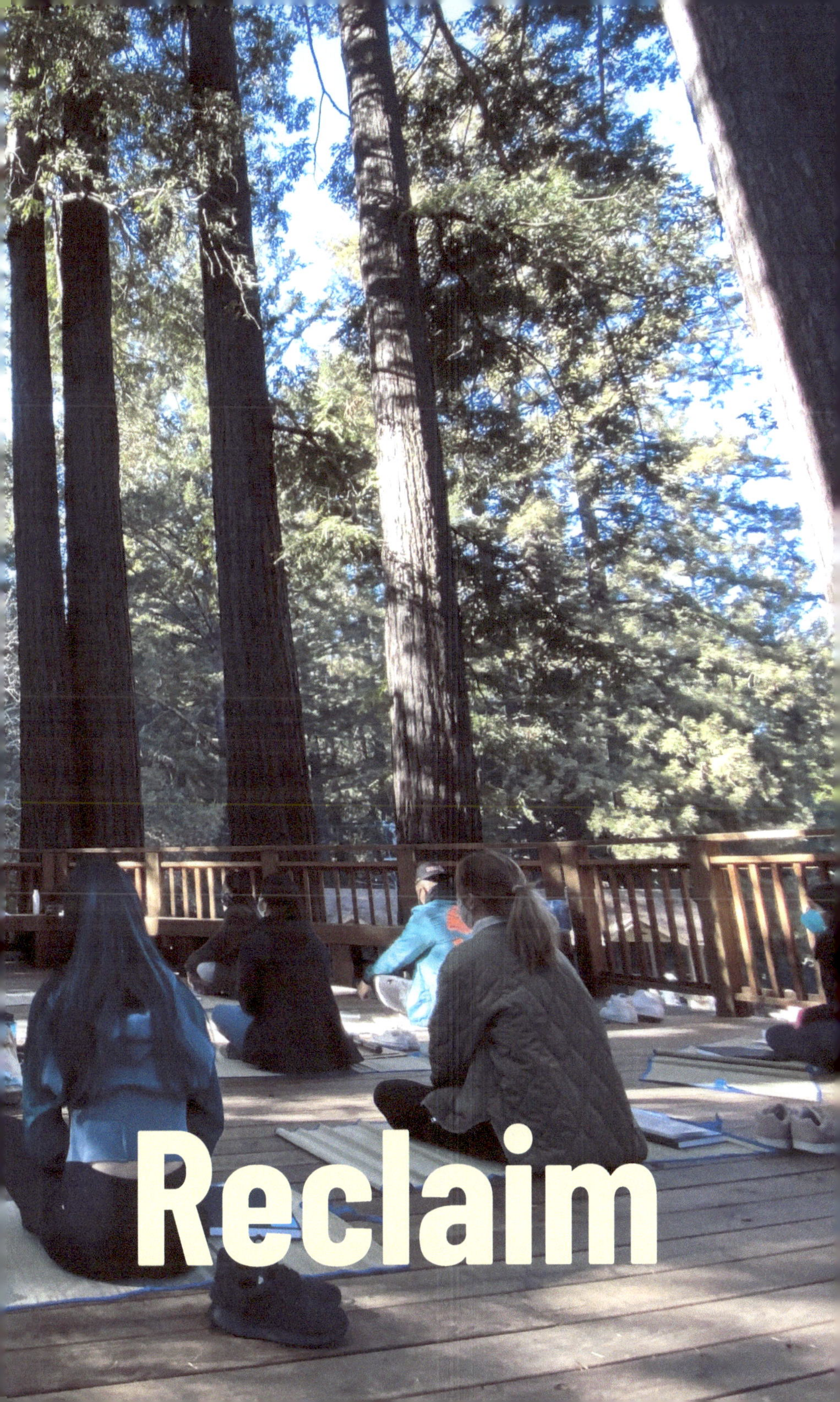

Reclaim

And So It Is
Poem by Lindsey Leong, aka HELLA famous

Priceless moments that don't crack

immortal like jade

allow our missteps to float away

clouds purge everything not meant for us

sun realigns us with our ancestral wisdom

it's not on us, it's in us

moon is coming home

a realignment to everything we are meant to be

and so it is....

we are Guan Yin

we are Buddha

we are God

we are awareness

we are transformative

we are water, endlessly pure, always moving...

the yin and yang

we are Heaven and Earth simultaneously

the teacher and the student

the grief and grieving

the love and loving

the healed and the healing

we are culture, we are community

as ever evolving questions we are the answer

together we are radical compassion in action

we are the question with the ultimate solution

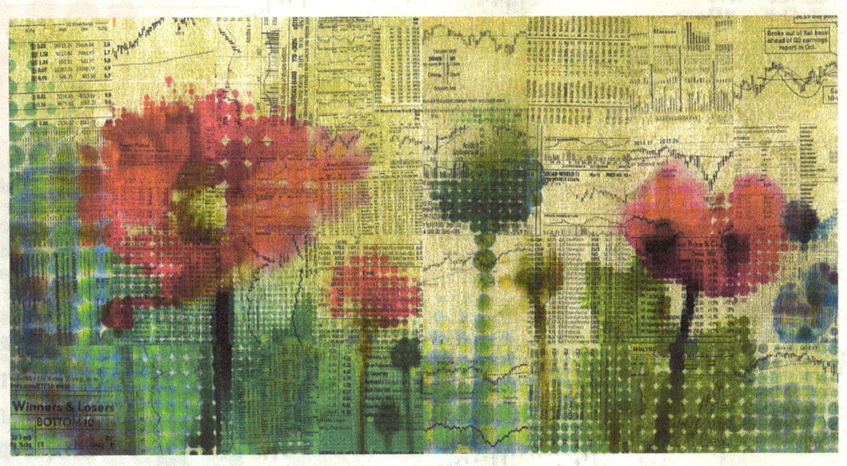

Phillip Hua, *Deciduous Deal,* UV cured acrylic print on acrylic with gold metal leafed panel, 2019

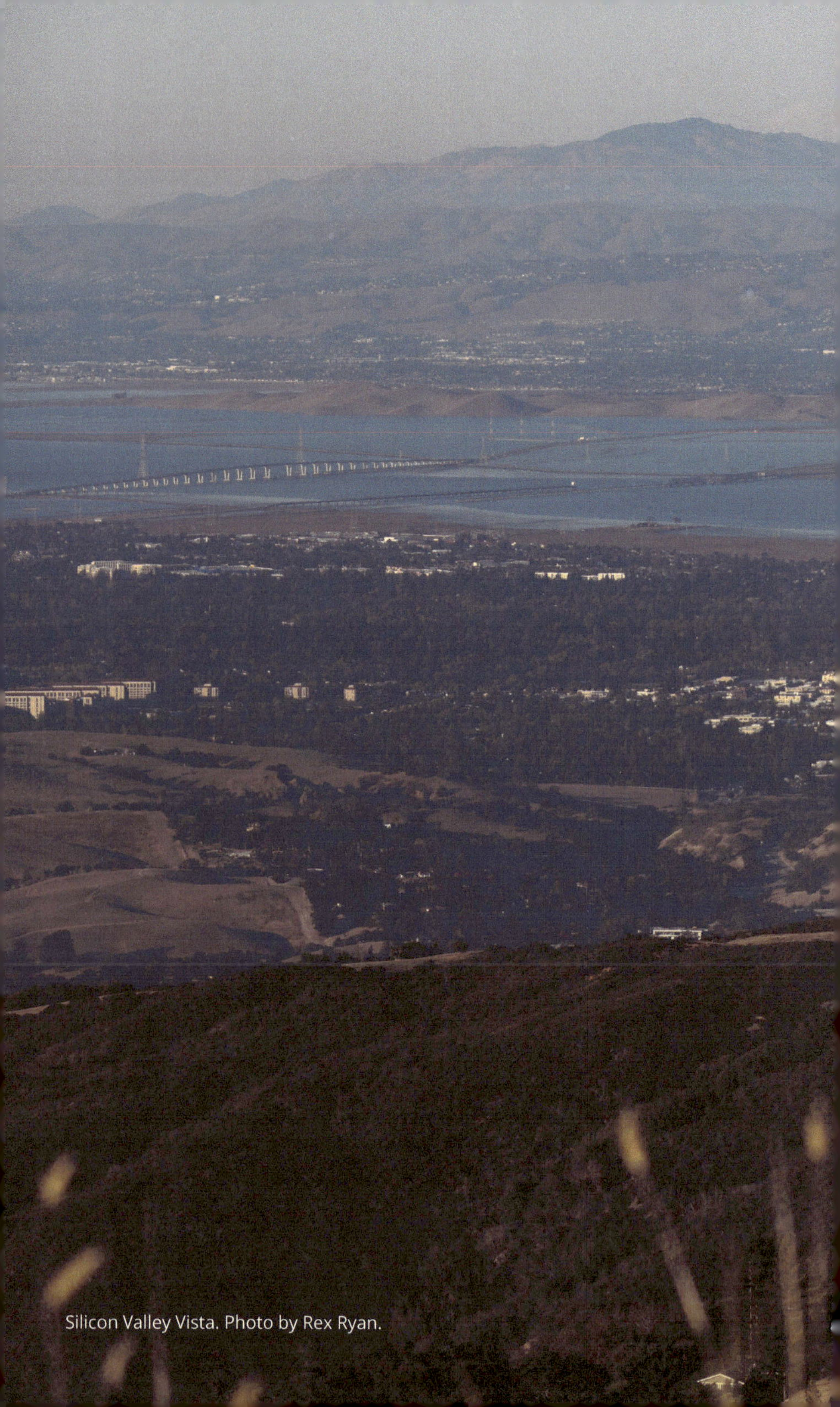

Silicon Valley Vista. Photo by Rex Ryan.

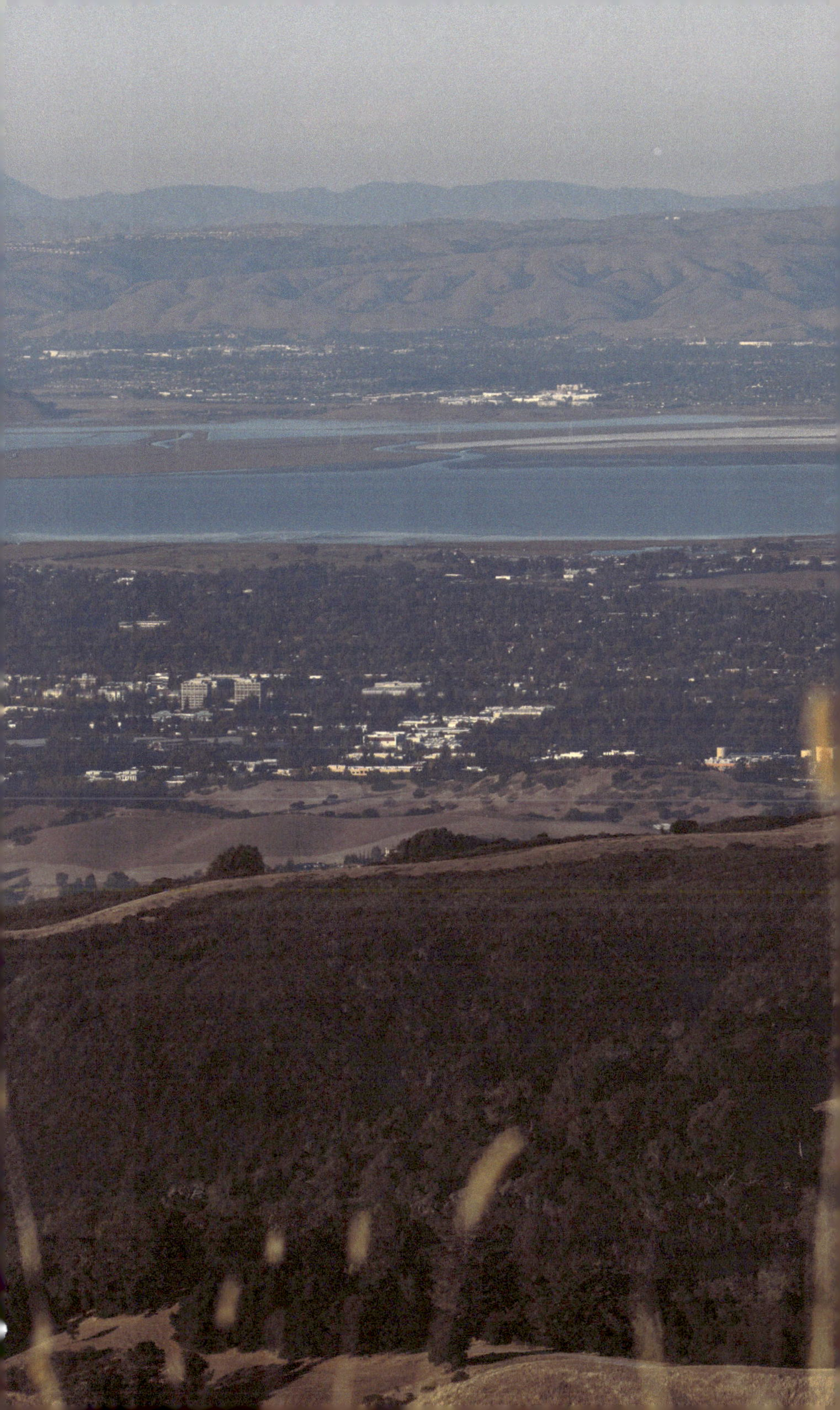

In Our Name
To L | Poem by Marisa Lin

林 : *woods; forest*

We follow trails through sun-cleaved
woods and peek behind trunks

braying their heights to sky. Birdsong
wraps its arms around our waists.

We dance, our steps teasing
trees awake, grandfathers

nudging grandmothers hoisting
cousins tickling infants

to see what we have brought them.
Joining our salsa, a black bear.

Then the moon pounding clouds
until all we hear is water

kissing water. No one to catch
this bright music but the earth,

her wrinkled hands fluttering
an immigrant country to orchestra

as she sews a name into bark,
character that spells a family

born from roots holding hands
below brilliant branches—

See brother, how they unwrap
our silence, make it fly.

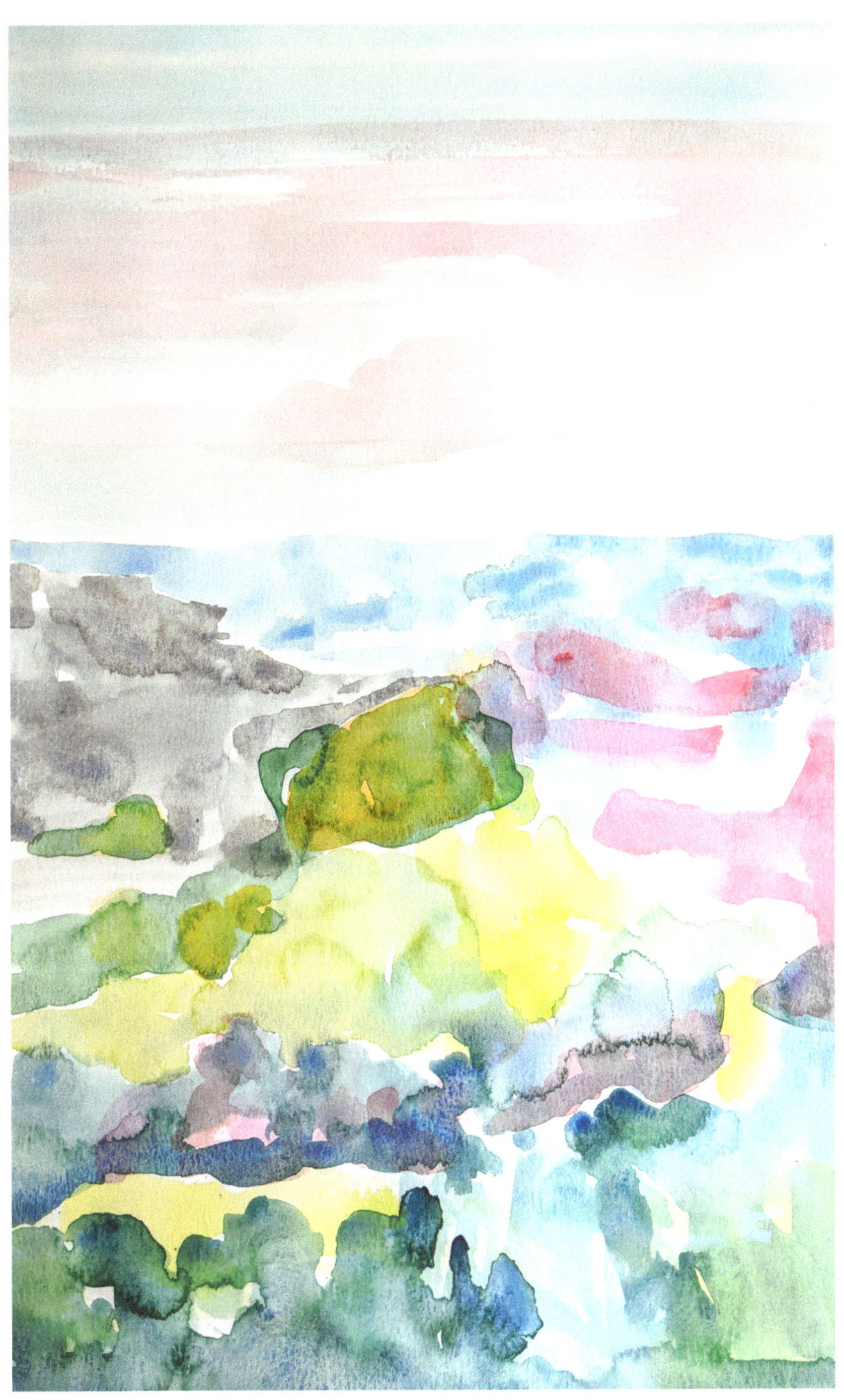

Cynthia Cao, *Mt. Umunhum #4*, watercolor on paper, 2018

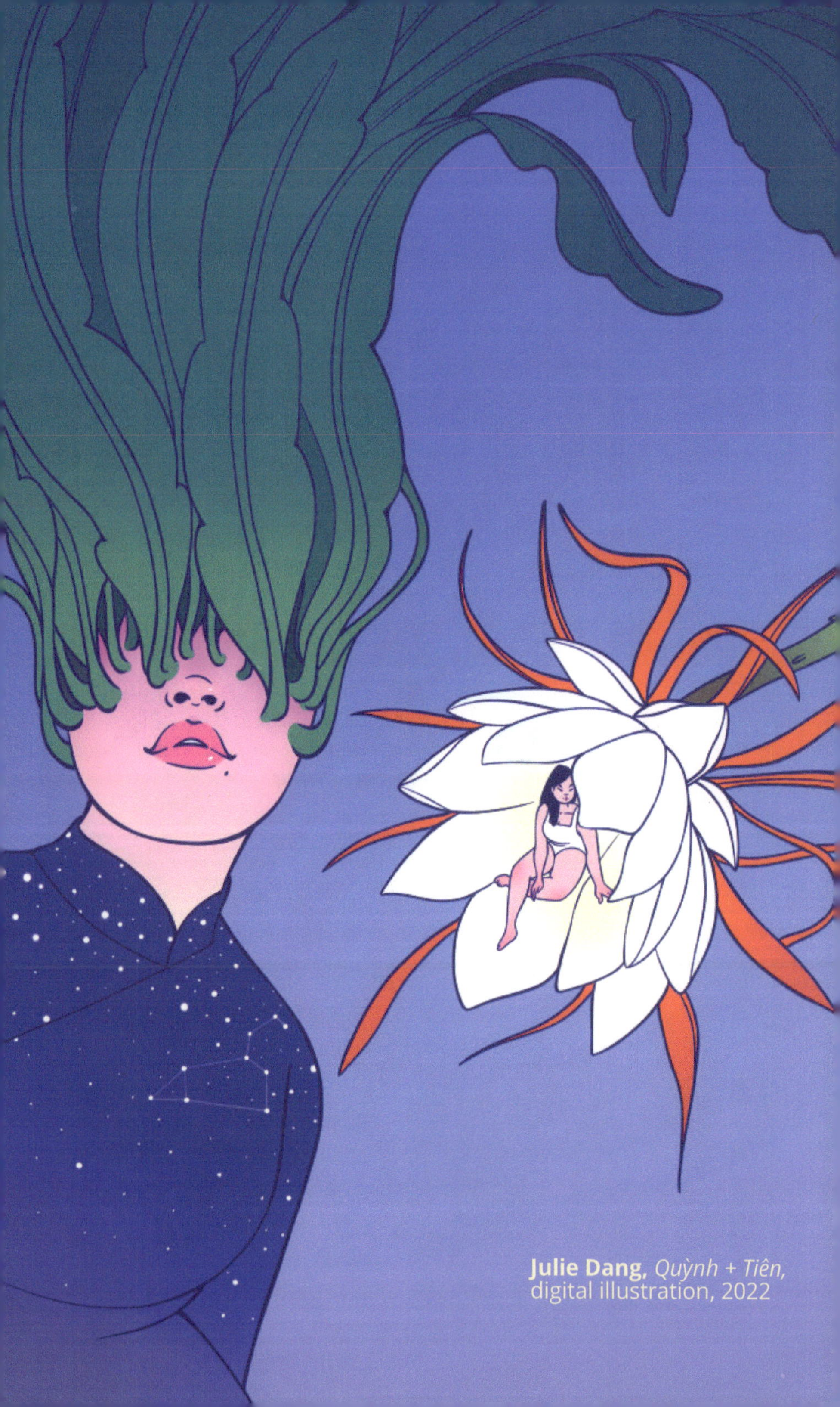

Julie Dang, *Quỳnh + Tiên,* digital illustration, 2022

Walk #1

WHAT'S IN A NAME?

Our names are a critical part of our identity given to us by our parents, grandparents, or family. They carry meaning and profound cultural, familial, and historical connections, and understanding. Our names identify the communities to which we belong.

Asians living in America often take on European-sounding names to avoid mispronunciations, misuse, or misgendering of our names. Though we accept these things will happen, it affects us deeply. It impacts our sense of belonging. Our names may trigger difficult and awkward situations, and we either correct or shrug off the misuse or mispronunciation to avoid making others feel bad. We are taught not to let others feel bad. We do so at our expense.

As you walk and enjoy the views, consider your name and ancestry.

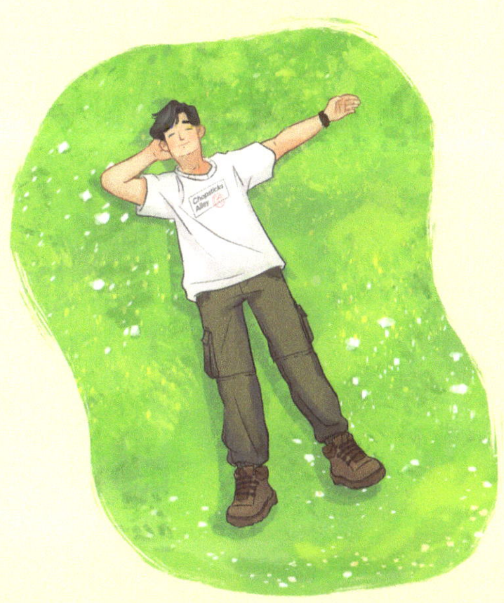

Meditation from Plum Village App

Select: Meditations > Guided Meditations > Short Meditations
Mindfulness of the Body by Brother Phap Dung (4:46 mins)

Select: Meditations > Guided Meditations > Touching the Earth
The Five Earth Touchings by Thich Nhat Hanh (6:21 mins)

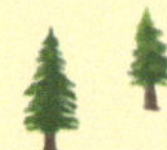

PARKS WITH INTERESTING NAMES

Sierra Azul Open Space Preserve at Mt. Umunhum
San Jose, CA 95120

Mt. Umunhum tops at 3,486 ft., making it the highest peak in the Santa Cruz mountain range. The Amah Mutsun Ohlone tribe has deep historical connections to this peak, as traditional stories tie the rise to the Amah Mutsun's discovery of fire. *Umunhum* is the Amah Mutsun word for the resting place of the hummingbird.

South Bay residents will recognize Mt. Umunhum by the tall concrete structure visible from the valley floor. Mt. Umunhum was formerly used as the Almaden Air Force Station, and the massive structure was a radar sail used during the Cold War.

You can find several parking lots on your drive up to the top of Mt. Umunhum: at the base (Jacques Ridge), at the midpoint (Bald Mountain), and at the summit (Mt. Umunhum summit). For panoramic views of the valley below, park at the Mt. Umunhum lot.

Arastradero Creek Loop 
Pearson-Arastradero Preserve,
1530 Arastradero Rd, Palo Alto, CA 94304

Arastradero Rd. was once a cattle trail; *Arastradero* in Spanish has several meanings: (1) a road used for logging; (2) pulling a dead bull with a rope; (3) coastal land gently sloping toward the sea, where ships were careened.

You'll find wildflowers, rolling grasslands, and an evergreen forest at this park. The park is open to hikers, bicyclists, and horseback riding, and is dog-friendly too! In 2022, POST saved a 13-acre island of land in the middle of the preserve from development. This park is a favorite for joggers and dog walkers, with a nice mix of rolling grassland and broadleaf evergreen forest.

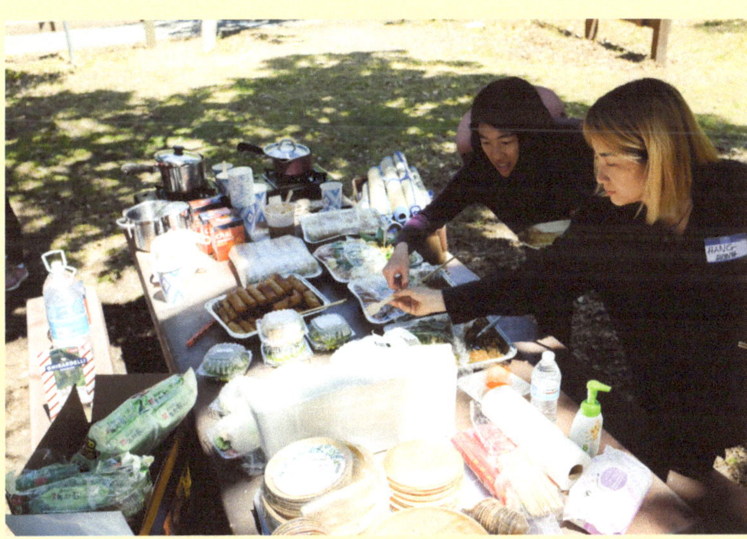

Asian American Healing Convening, May 2022, Alum Rock Park.
Photo by Martin Mijares.

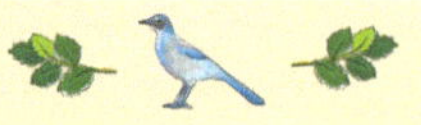

Write a poem following Koel's poetry tradition.
Koel tradition comes from Southeast Asia and the Pacific.
It is a three-line poem in which the first and third lines rhyme, and the second line uses alliteration.
Example:

Give all your worries to the sky
creating contagious courage
so your highest self will fly

- Lindsey Leong, aka HELLA famous

Reflect on your name and reclaim your sense of self.

Prompt #1:
Think about these questions:
Where did my name come from?
What is its history?
What does being in harmony in all parts of me feel like?
What are some things I can do today to honor my whole being?

Prompt #2:

Write or draw your story.
What's a big challenge you overcame?
How did you find strength in this part of your journey?
What did you learn about yourself, and what can you honor about yourself?

Prompt #3:

List five things that help you feel happy with yourself today.

Self-care Tips

- Positive affirmations are positive phrases or statements used to challenge negative thoughts when they arise.
- Write a phrase that resonates with you.
- Repeat it three to four times a day.

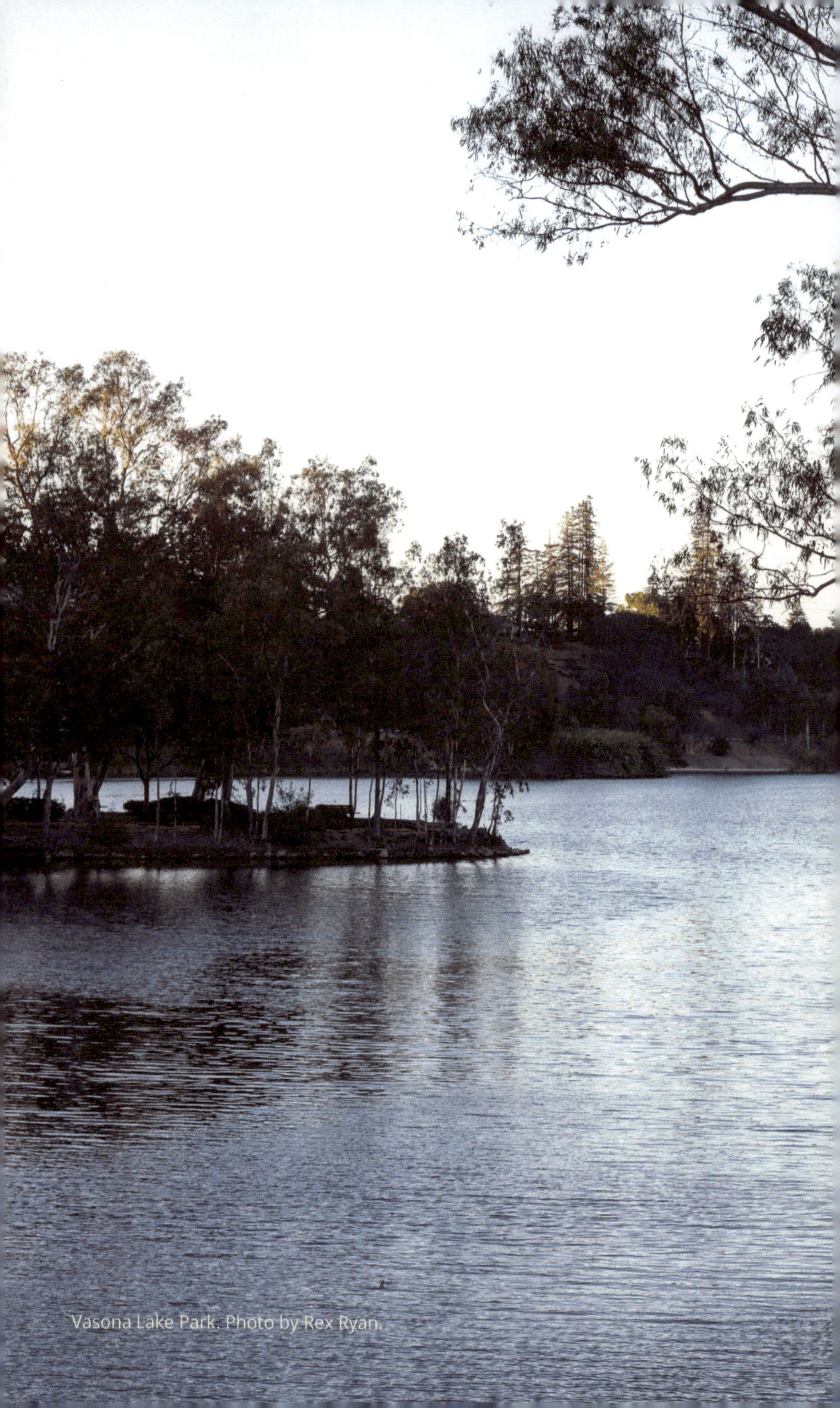

Vasona Lake Park. Photo by Rex Ryan.

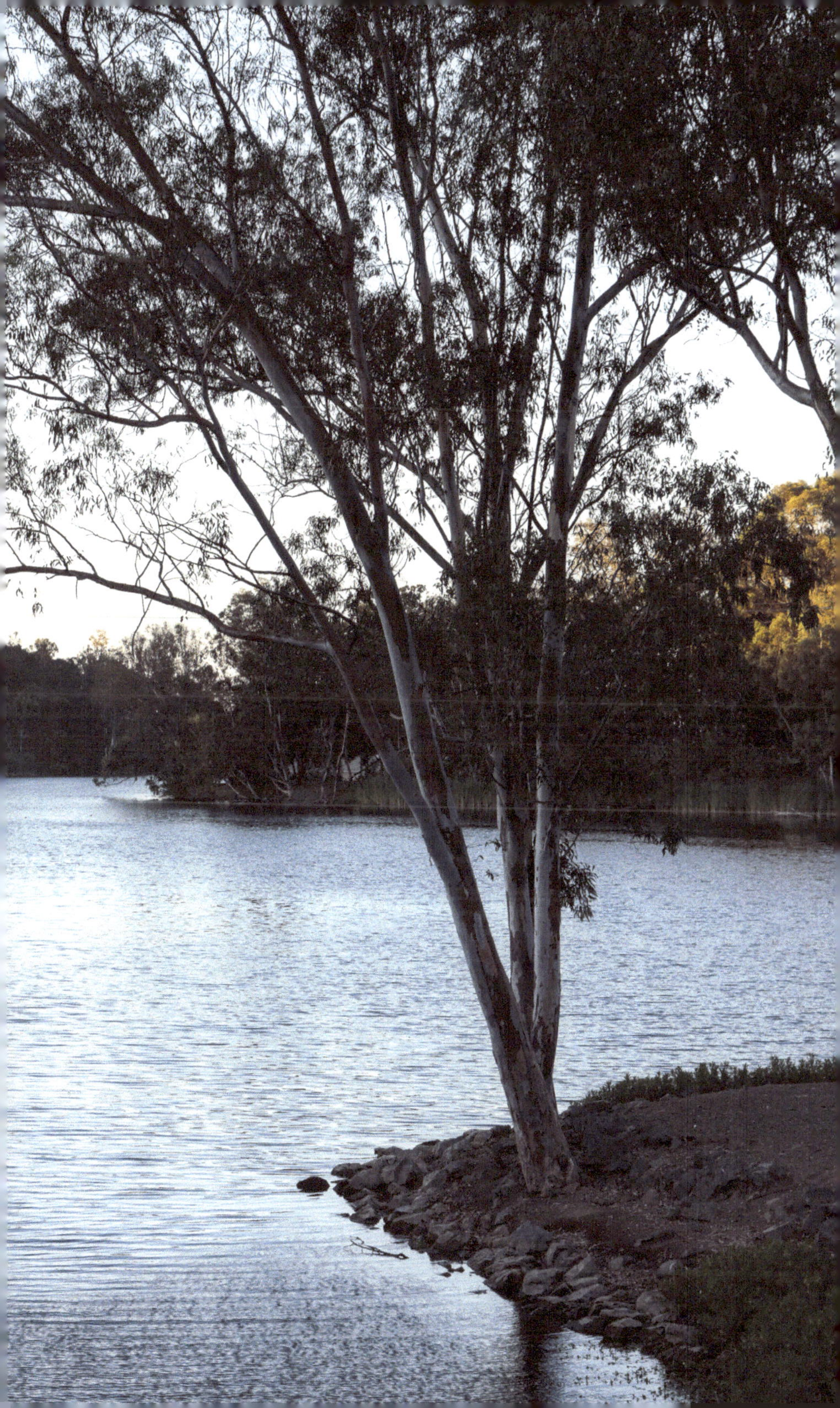

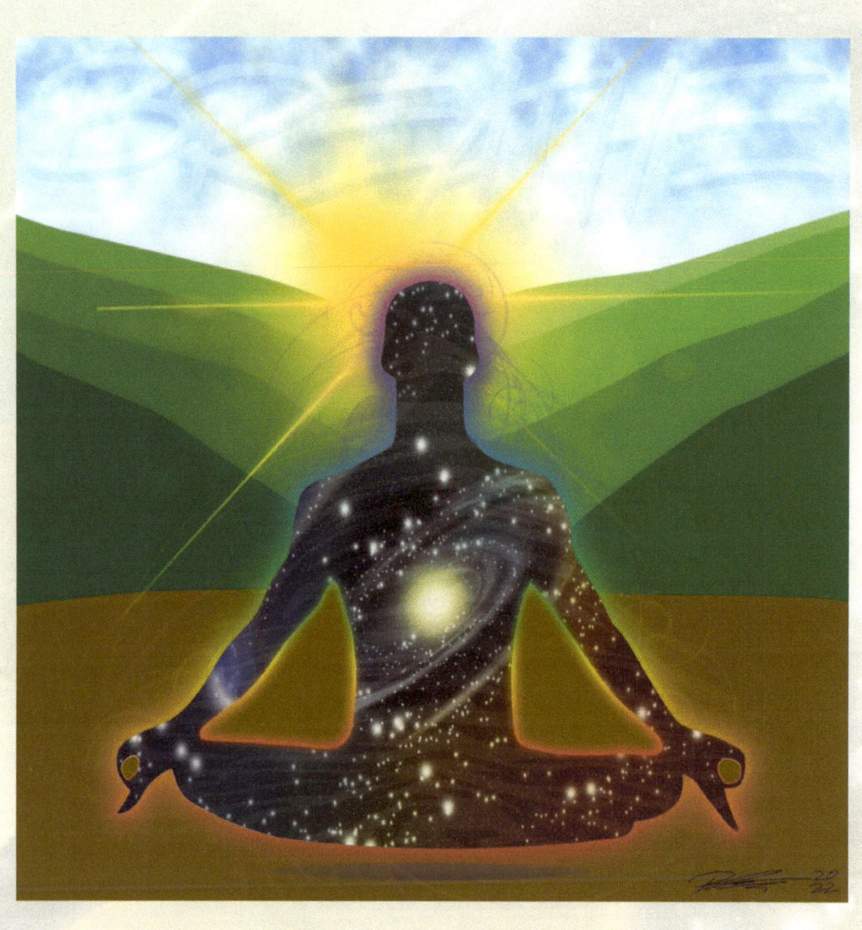

Rey Simpauco, *Breathe*, digital illustration, 2022

Laundry and Taxes
Poem by Yan-Yin Choy

A storm of emotions sweeping through the golden mountains,
I am the moonlit tumultuous tide,
rolling in and reflecting deep, deep joy,
rolling out and reflecting deep, deep sorrow.

I am the swaying bay laurel trees that thrums and bends,
a spicy aroma wafting into my nostrils.

I am the wave that dances under the moonlight,
unlearning the colonial myth
that I am undeserving of rest, celebration, and support.

I am the sweet, soft lush native grass,
a cushion for your fall on your family hikes.

I am the flap of dragon wings ushering forth rain on the Ohlone land,
waterfalls flowing heavier, like the roaring sound of my heartbeat post-heartbreak:
growing stronger.

I am the unbounded possibility of future,
my ancestors' wildest dreams unleashed.

I am the fragrant incense and plume of smoke drifting through the air,
as we pay homage with offerings
of sweet and fluffy Char Siu Bao,
of crispy roast duck,
of strong Iron Goddess tea, and
of steamed shiitake mushrooms, snap peas, and bok choy,
all for my elders in the spiritual realm.

I am the abyss of memory,
secrets collected under the watchful eye of forests and mountains on Ohlone land.

I am the kaleidoscope of soft sunset, every color representing the variations of my
life in the multiverse.

I am the vast salt marshes, with bay tides gently dancing under the sunset,
grounded in the love abundant in my life,
I embrace that *this* is the universe where I'm meant to be.

I am the glow of containing all of this turmoil,
Alchemizing into a flock of marsh wrens, singing their playful songs,
soaring high, high, high.

Walk #2

WE ARE WHAT WE EAT

For this walk, try to engage your five senses: sight, hearing, smell, touch, and taste. Eating together is not a formalized process; food can evoke memories of the past and is a conduit to emotions that are special to us, the ones we hold close to our hearts. Food reminds us of our culture, roots, identity, and fond moments with the people we love. As our ancestors did, you will experience joy and release through sharing food, conversation, and reconnecting with others.

Pack a lunch and invite your loved ones to have a picnic.

Meditation from Plum Village App

Select: Meditations > Eating Meditations
Coffee or Tea Meditation by Brother Phap Linh (6:24 mins)
Eating Meditation by Brother Phap Linh (5:18 mins)

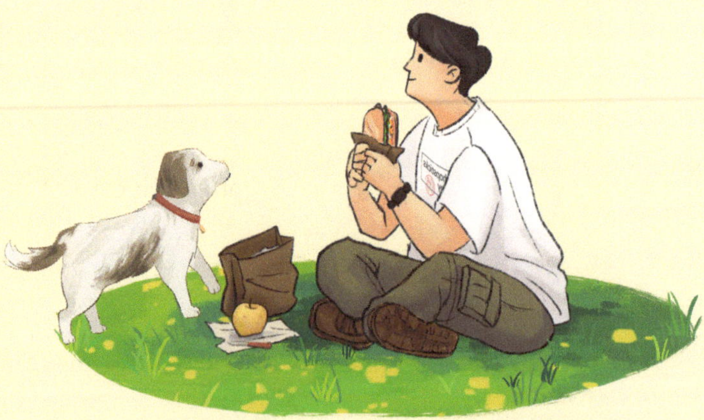

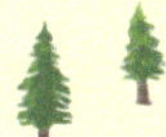

PARKS PERFECT FOR PICNICS

Vasona Lake County Park
333 Blossom Hill Rd Los Gatos, CA 95032

This park offers 45 acres of grassy lawn where you can picnic, practice yoga, and play games. The Los Gatos Creek trail runs through the park and is available to joggers, cyclists, and dog owners alike!

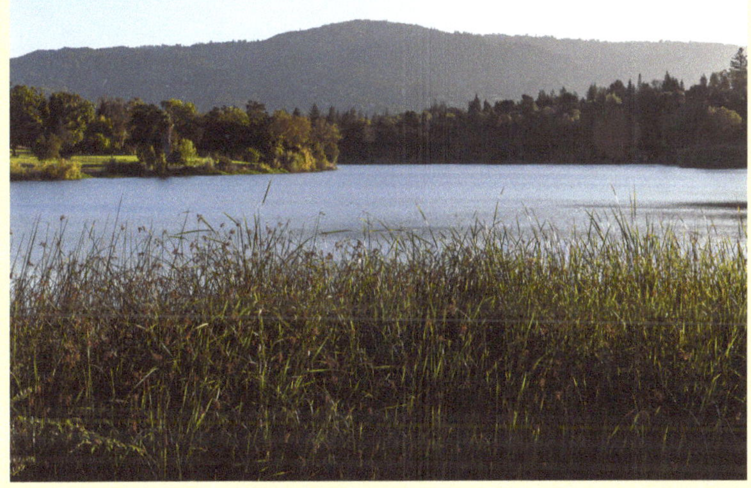

Vasona Lake Park. Photo by Rex Ryan.

In the adjoining Oak Meadow Park, a carousel and a steam-powered engine operated by Billy Jones Wildcat Railroad takes visitors through both parks. Paddle and row boats are available through Los Gatos Recreation for rent from Spring to Fall.

Vasona Lake County Park also participates in the Agents of Discovery educational mobile game app, where participants walk through the park and answer questions about the park's history, local wildlife, and the surrounding ecosystem.

Picnic tables are available on a first-come, first-served basis with a three-table limit. Large group events can be accommodated by reserving a group picnic area at **gooutsideandplay.org**. The parking fee is $6.

Sanborn County Park
16055 Sanborn Rd Saratoga, CA 95070

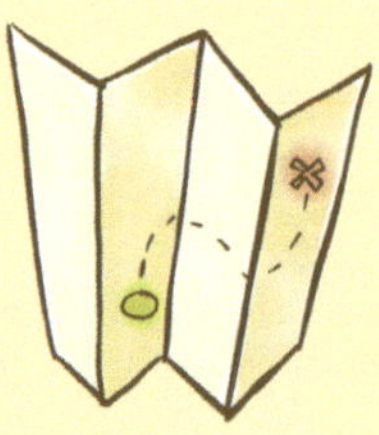

Sanborn County Park is 3,453 acres of protected land with a 40-acre day-use area perfect for people to picnic and enjoy time outdoors. Black-tailed deer are frequently seen foraging in the grassy areas of the park.

The park features 22 miles of hiking trails and offers RV camping year-round and hike-in camping from March through October. During the summer, the theater is home to **Silicon Valley Shakespeare**, a non-profit company offering the playwright's work in an intimate outdoor setting.

For an easy, mostly flat hike under the shade of trees, take the *Sunnyvale Mountain Trailhead* north to the *Skyline Trailhead*, which will connect *Indian Rock* (3 miles), known for its massive sandstone features, for an out-and-back hike of 6 miles total. The parking fee is $6.

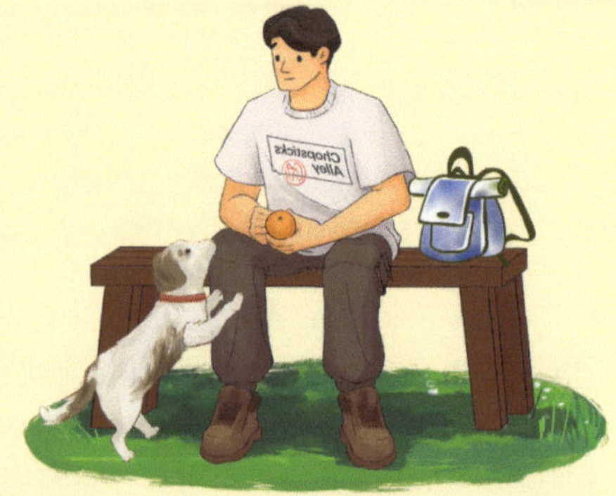

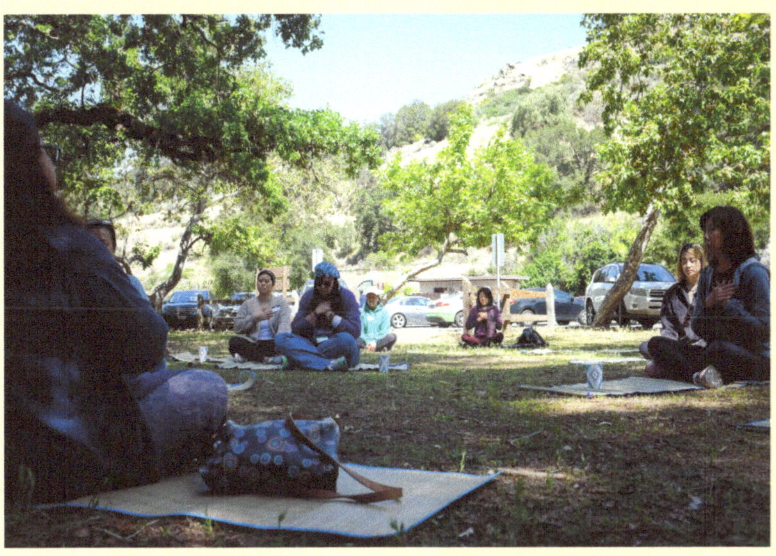

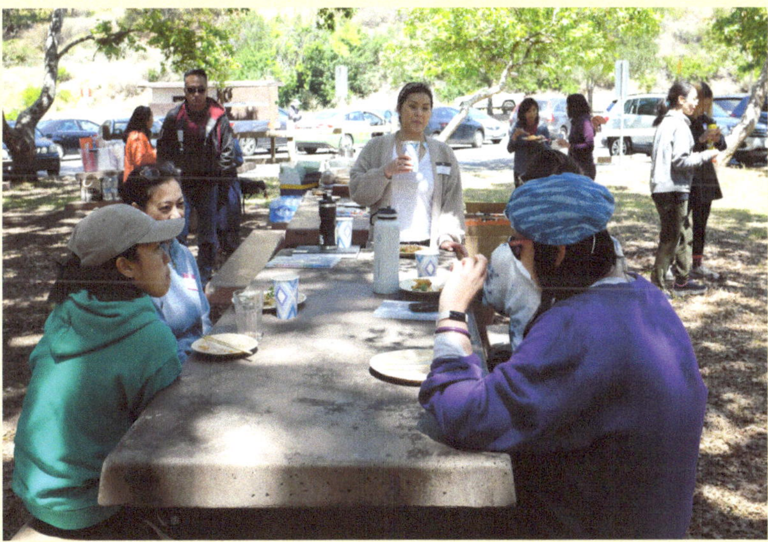

Asian American Healing Convening, May 2022, Alum Rock Park.
Photos by Martin Mijares.

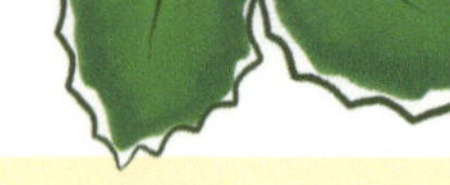

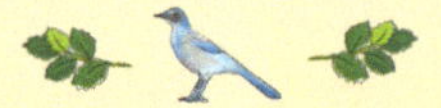

Write a poem following Kural's poetry tradition.

Kural is a poetry tradition from India and Sri Lanka with only two lines. The first line has four words, and the second line has three.

Example:

Mindful manifesting movement making
marathons for restoration

- Lindsey Leong, aka HELLA famous

Reconnect with your culture, ancestors, and community.

Prompt #1:

Reflect on the following questions:

What stories have you been accepting about your culture when you were young? Are they still true or not?

How would you rewrite these stories to create more acceptance of your ancestry?

Self-care Tips

- Take a break from your computer or phone and connect with people or pets that you love and care about.
- Stay away from things and people that drain your energy and make you feel bad about yourself.

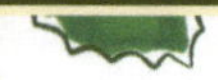

Prompt #2:

Write a loving letter or draw an image of your life from the future as if you were already there. Share some wisdom you want to tell your younger self.
What would your future self say to your current self to help you be at peace today?

Prompt #3:

List five things that nourish your body, mind, or heart. Commit to one and indulge in that nourishing thought or action today.

Group Activity

This exercise is intended for your group to be childlike, having fun eating, making art, or writing poetry together, and spending time in gratitude.

- Gather your group for a short meditation to reconnect with nature, your bodies, and minds.
- Have your group contribute to a Community Table: Participants may share food or drinks, a drawing, an object found in nature, or a positive phrase of gratitude.

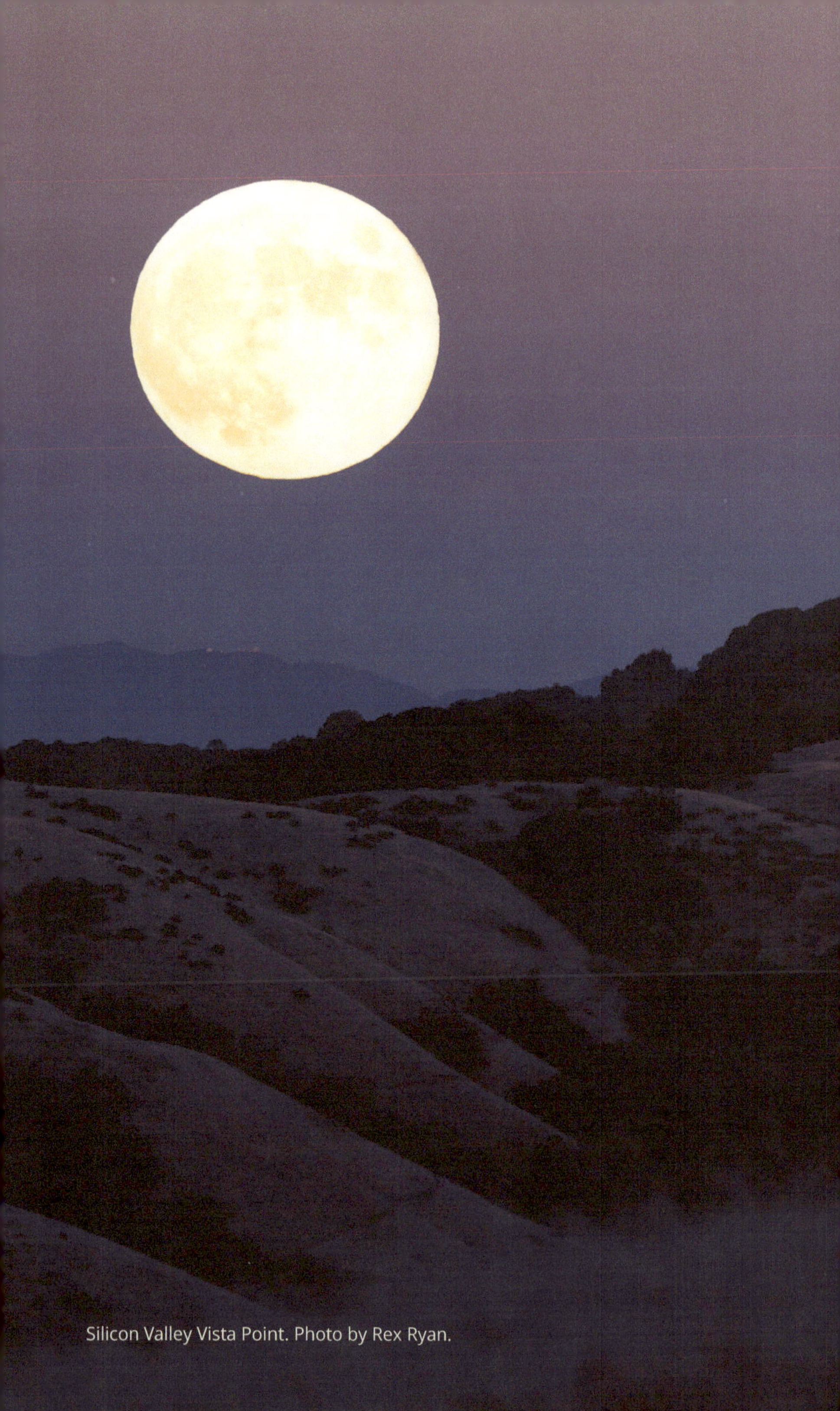
Silicon Valley Vista Point. Photo by Rex Ryan.

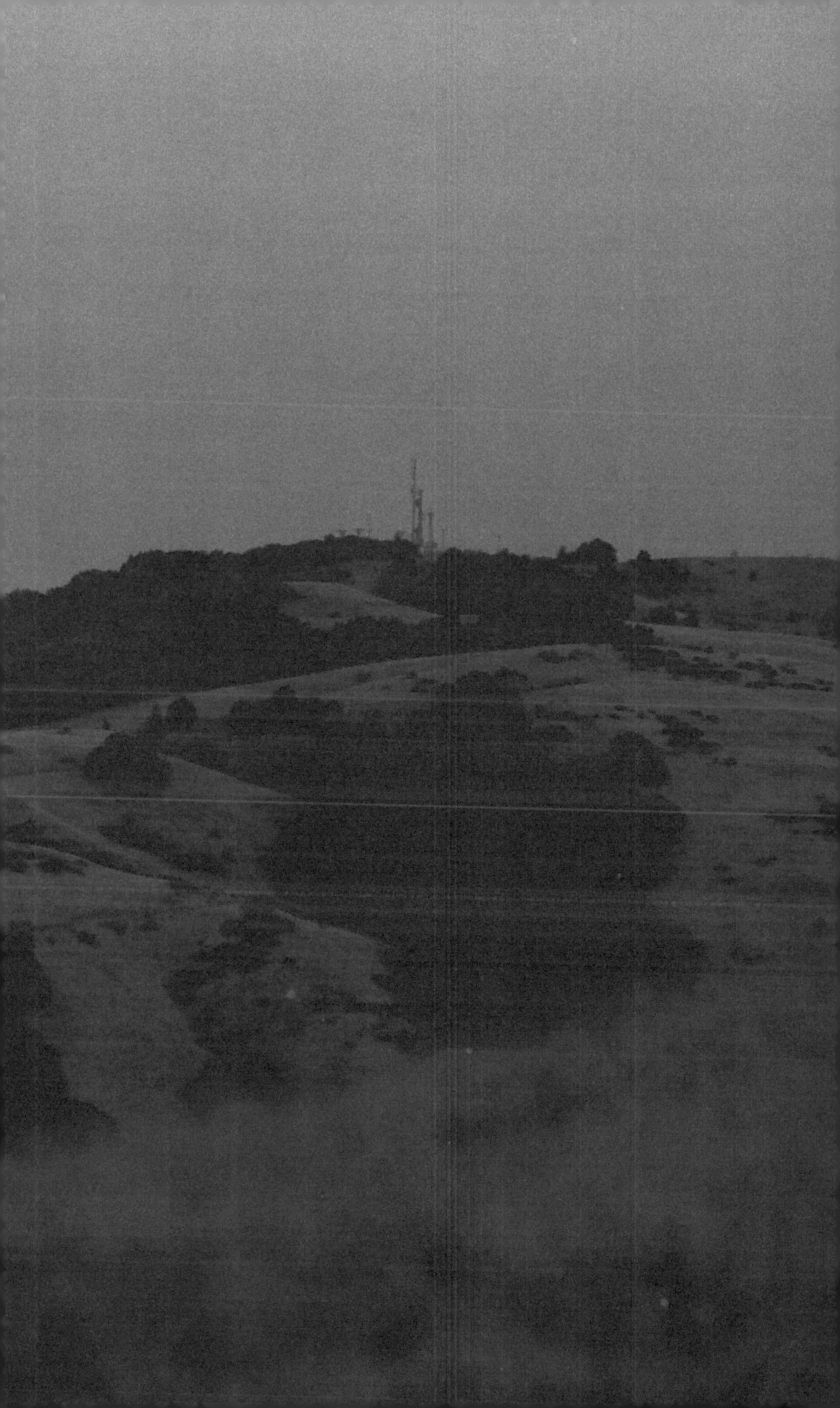

Memories
Poem by Hang Huynh

Thought this would be forever
Seemed like yesterday
Together we were
Moon, I called her
The light of my tree, my life
Forever will be

Gone, you are gone
Like the wind
Forever gone
Just she and I
Here we will be
Forever here

Stand
No matter what
I will stand
Because of her
The light my tree, my life
Forever she and I
Together we stand

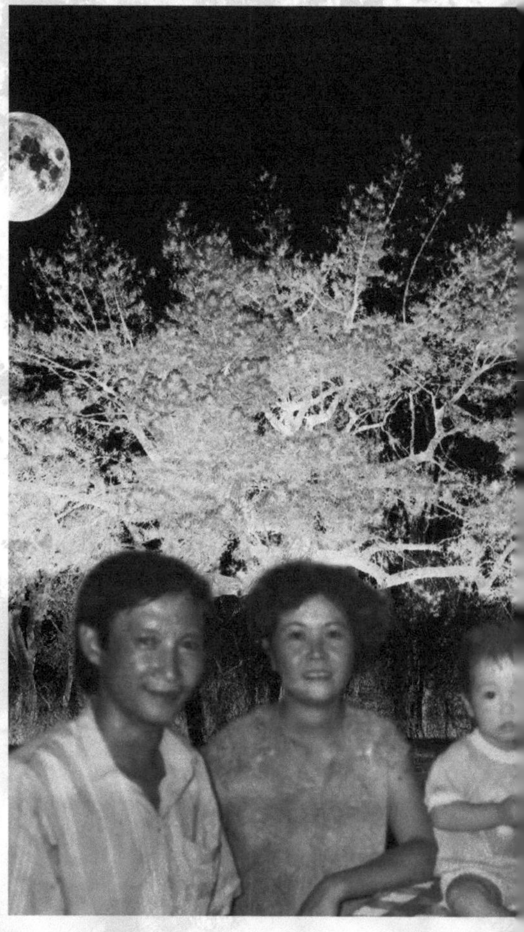

Persistent I must be
Won't be scared
Won't be hurt
Will be quick and time will fly
We will be fine
Together we'll be

"Hey, I am here
Sitting, waiting, and wishing
Could we ever come back
The time we were
For one last chance..."

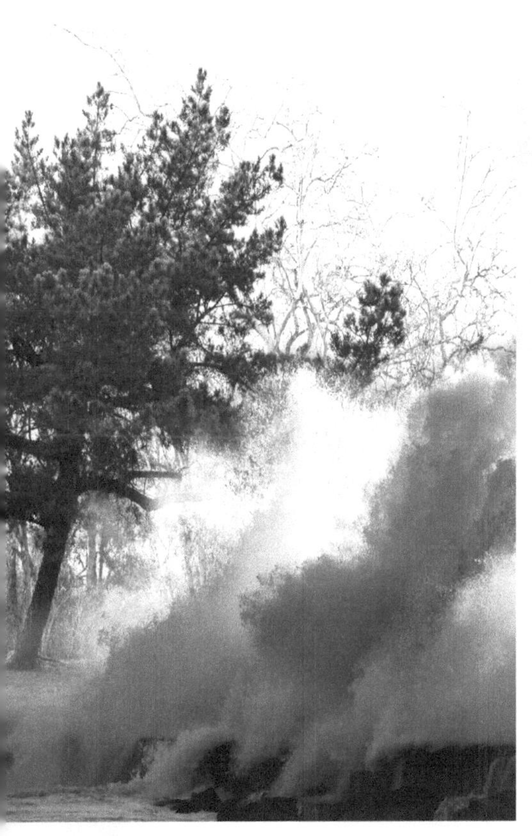

What if we are still here
Could we be a perfect family
Or a broken one?
As old as we are
Is everything still the same?
Calm and infinite
It's just a thought
If we are still here...

(left) **Hang Huynh**, *In My Memory*, digital photo collage, 2023
(right) **Hang Huynh**, *New Beginning*, digital photo collage, 2023

Walk #3

WALK WITH THE MOON

The moon is associated with gentleness and brightness in Chinese and Vietnamese cultures. The round shape symbolizes family reunions. The full moon is a representation of abundance, harmony, and good luck.

Experience a sense of community through sharing every day experiences and stories. By showing gratitude to our ancestors who endured so much to pave the way for us, we are grounding ourselves. Being emotionally whole is to surround ourselves with trustworthy connections and be a dependable connection for others.

To that end, gratitude is the path to wholeness.

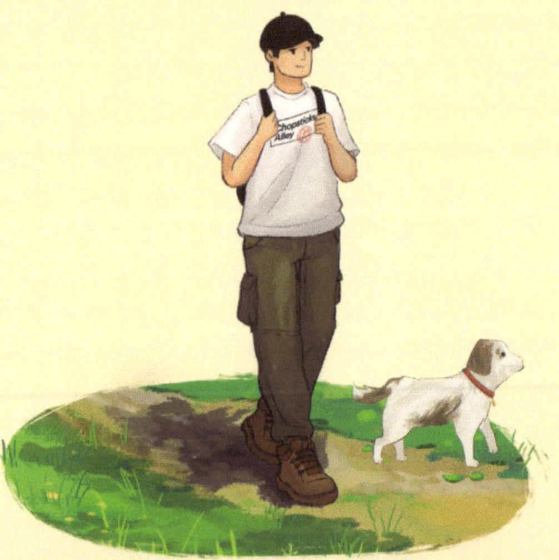

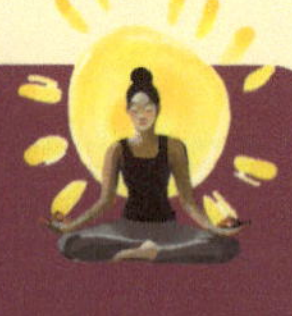

Meditation from Plum Village App

Select: Meditations > Guided Meditations > Short Meditations
Calm - Ease by Sister Peace (6:07 mins)

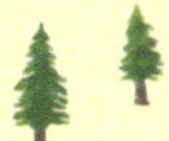

PARKS TO VIEW THE MOON

Silicon Valley Vista Point
20001-20039 Skyline Blvd, Redwood City, CA 94062

Located off Skyline Boulevard, this vista point faces east overlooking Silicon Valley with panoramic views to the North and South. Across the valley is the Diablo Mountain Range with the Sierra Foothills beneath them.

This site is next to the Russian Ridge Open Space Preserve. It is perfect for taking an afternoon hike and then jumping back in the car for snacks, and a front-row seat to view the moon in all its stages.

Dumbarton Bridge via Shoreline Trail Parking
808 Marshlands Rd, Fremont, CA 94555

This location allows you to take in the views of the moon from down in the valley. It is on the *Shoreline Trail*, which runs parallel to the Dumbarton Bridge.

Note that you must pay the toll if you cross the bridge traveling East to West from 680/880. Instead, from San Jose, take 101 North and exit Willow Rd, then 84 East to Marshlands Rd. to avoid the toll.

If you plan your trip for the late afternoon or evening, pack layers of clothing to protect yourself from the wind and cooler temperatures.

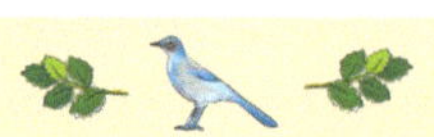

Write a poem following Sijo's poetry tradition.

Sijo is a traditional three-line poem from Korea that is 14-16 syllables per line. The first line introduces the subject, the second line develops the subject, and the third and final line is the twist. Example:

Lotus radiating sacred words and actions of healing
the harvest moon illuminating peaceful blessings of reunion
no mud, no lotus, no sun, no moon, the interbeing of the sacred

- Lindsey Leong, aka HELLA famous

Now it's your turn. Trust your wisdom to guide you.

Prompt #1:

Reflect on the following questions:
Who do you feel most connected to who is no longer alive?
What do they want you to see or experience?
What wisdom and grace can you take away from this experience?

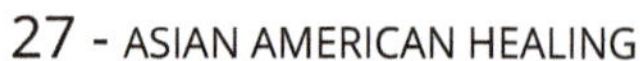

Prompt #2

Write or draw: What are you grateful for? What message do you wish for your ancestors and spirit guides to read or see?

Prompt #3

List five ways that you've been a light to others.

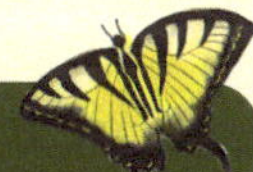

Self-care Tips

Positive psychology focuses on what is going right rather than wrong. The Three Blessings is an intervention adapted from Martin Seligman, known as the father of Positive Psychology. This specific type of journaling has helped people to be in tune with or attend to optimistic feelings.

Instructions:

- Every day, for the next seven days, before going to bed, think about three good things that have happened each day (big or small).
- Write it out with as many details as possible.
- Why do you think it happened?
- How did it make you feel?

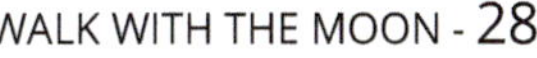

Castle Rock. Photo by Rex Ryan.

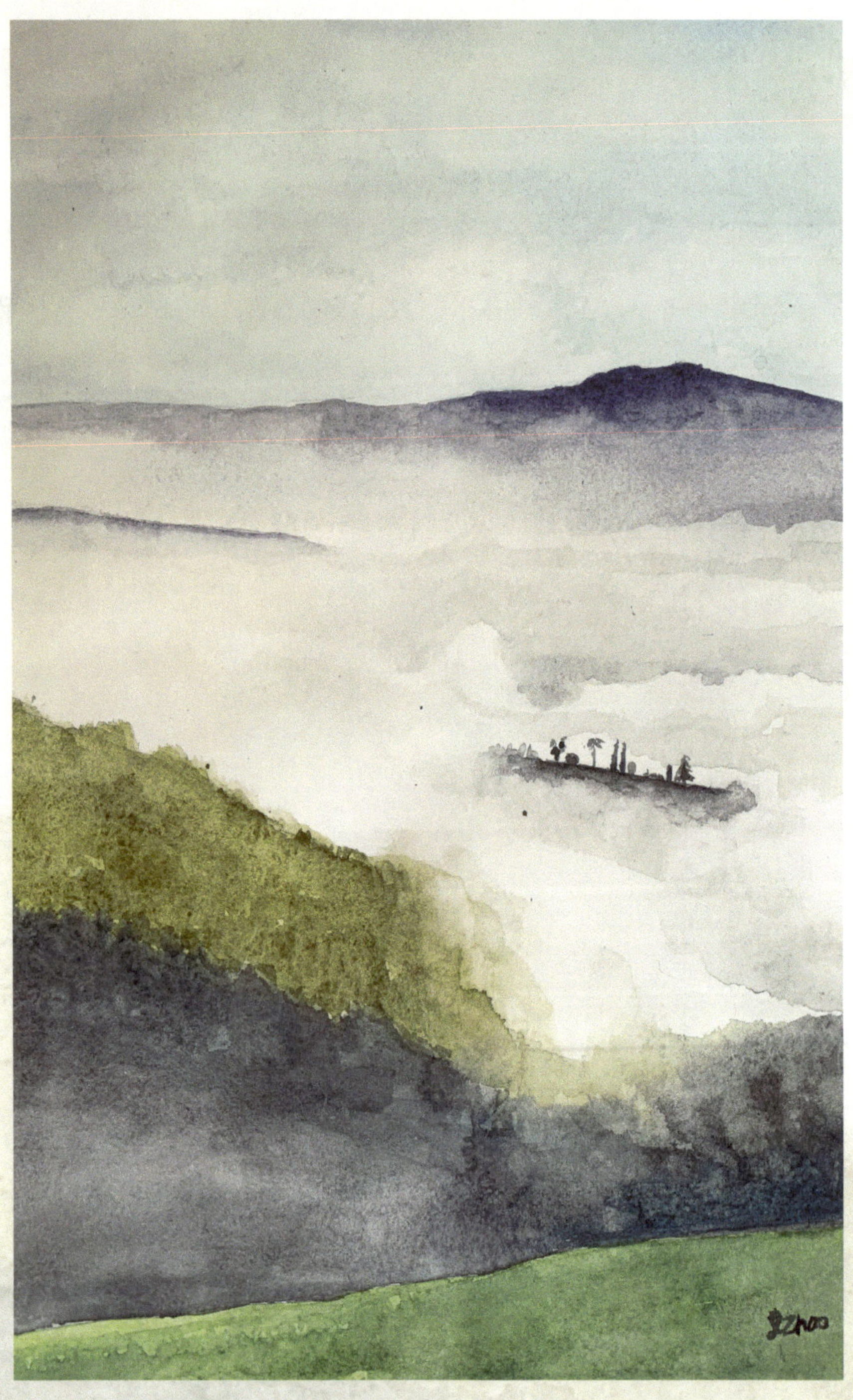

Louisa Zhao, *Misty Morning in the Bay,* watercolor, 2022

Epistula Heroidi (Letter to a Heroine)
Poem by Brian Le

Mẹ ơi,
Dear Mom,   do you ever turn your thoughts back
                                        to your quê hương
                                        homeland?
Vietnam, your country with its fragrance
            your quê   hương
You recall

                        sometimes   warm tropical air
the delicate aroma of hoa ngọc lan
                                the jade orchid flower
scent subtle   petals slender   smooth white, as

—pure white as a girl's áo dài uniform at your school
in Saigon, next to the temple, where blossoms of
hoa ngọc lan scatter their holy blessings of prosperity—

sudden hot rain   asphalt steam
                        stink of fish market
night sky flashing above   bomb shelter below
                        rancid stench of sandbags
life goes on   war relentless

now, on a distant shore, waters of the same ocean
but far from the waters of Sông Hương
                                the Perfume River

            nothing left of your quê hương
except   language culture family
            and your collection of stamps—
never to be sent, not to mark letters, but memories—
in your single bag, taken as you fled Vietnam
                                facing
hardship and struggle   with courage and resilience
                        light and optimism
            the name Anh Thư
                        a Heroine, sign of who you are to me
            so I send you this letter
                                lá thư to hold your memories—
—now my memories—of a quê hương I have never known.

Walk #4

I AM WATER

In Taoism, water is the soothing, relaxing release of tension that occurs with the stilling of the overactive body and mind while bringing out its hidden strengths.

In early India, powerful goddesses were represented by water. Water was celebrated and worshiped as a purificatory substance, but it was also characterized as potentially dangerous or violent.

Water plays a vital role in Thai culture. It symbolizes not only fertility and refreshment but also prosperity and purification.

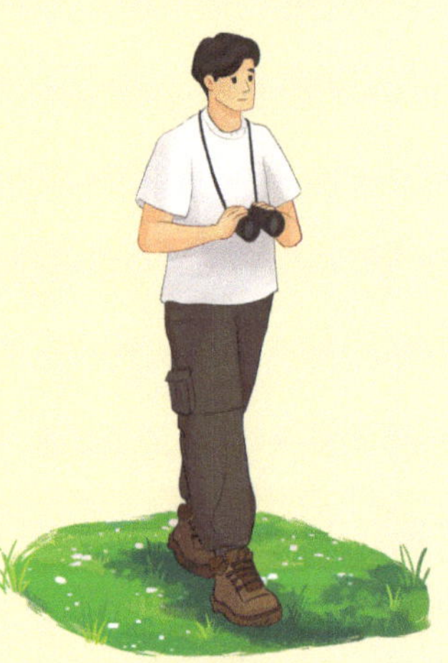

To experience a new start, allow the sound of water to wash over you or take a dip in it when possible.

*Check out Songkran to learn why the Thai New Year is celebrated in April.

Meditation from Plum Village App

Select: Meditations > Guided Meditations > Earth Contemplations
Mother of all Beings written by Thich Nhat Hanh, read by Sister True Dedication (4:37 mins)
Walking Tenderly written by Thich Nhat Hanh, read by Sister True Dedication (5:56 mins)

Bonus Meditations
Select: *Listening to the Rain Veranda* to find different water sounds and meditations

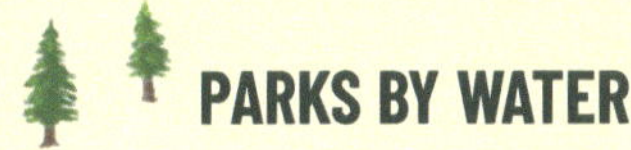

PARKS BY WATER

Pillar Point Bluff
Parking lot, Airport St. Moss Beach, CA 94038

This coast side trail offers ocean views and views of the surrounding bluffs, farmlands, and harbor. The radar tower at Pillar Point, Air Force Station, is visible as you hike this easy, flat trail crisscrossing the coastal preserve.

Take the trail 1.5 miles south toward the Pillar Point station and stop by Half Moon Bay Brewing Company or Barbara's Fishtrap for a nice sit-down meal. After lunch, walk down to the jetty to dig your toes in the sand and take in the fresh ocean breeze.

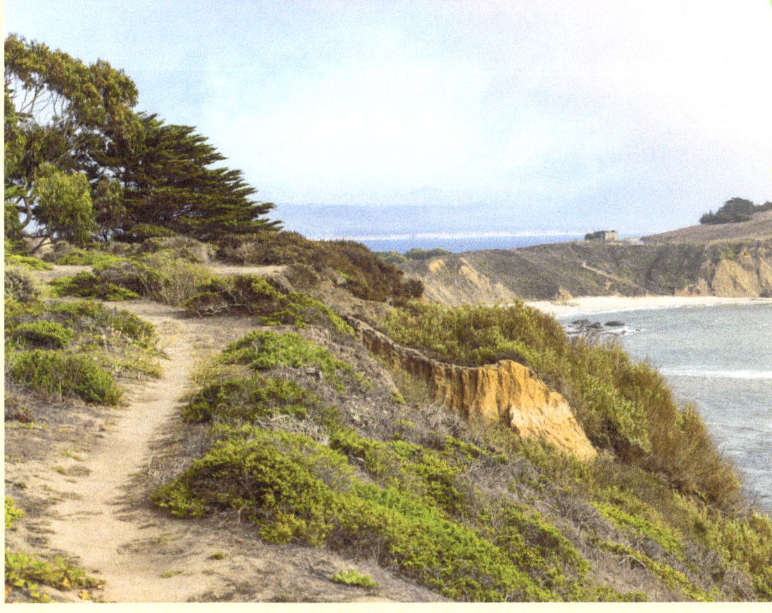

Pillar Point Bluff. Photo by Rex Ryan.

Castle Rock State Park
15000 Skyline Boulevard Los Gatos, CA 95030

Popular among rock climbers, this state park is known for its sandstone rock formations surrounded by bay laurel, black oak, knob-cone pine, and coast redwoods in the Santa Cruz Mountain range.

From the main entrance at Skyline Boulevard, follow the *Saratoga Gap Trail* to the *Interconnector Trail* and *Ridge Trail*.

Castle Rock Falls has a lookout platform allowing visitors to see various rock formations, redwood forest groves, and the waterfall fed by natural springs that feed into the San Lorenzo River 75 feet below.

There is also a popular climbing route next to the falls; visitors may see local climbers tackling the course depending on the day.

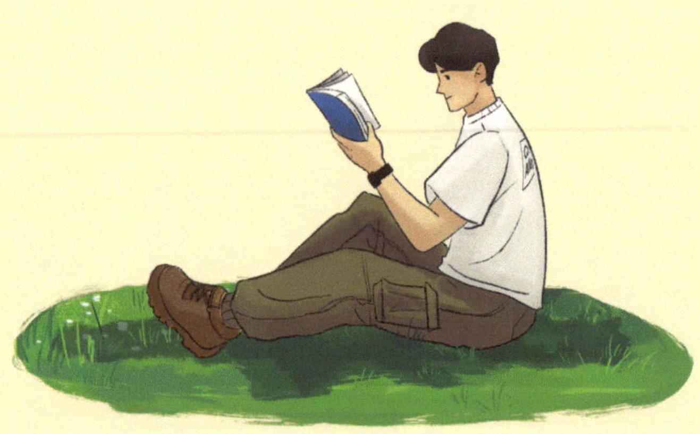

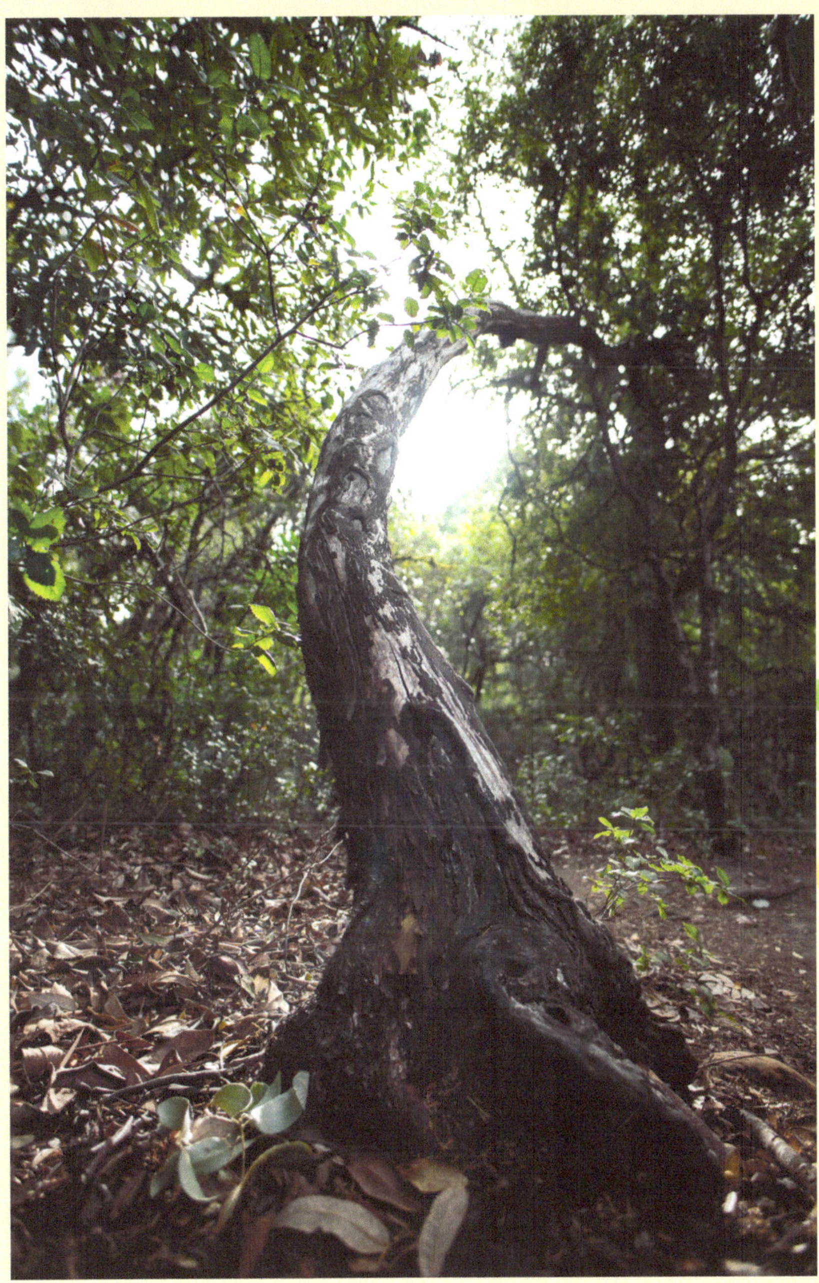

Castle Rock State Park. Photo by Rex Ryan.

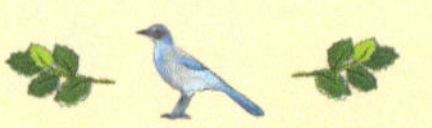

Write a poem following Syair's poetry tradition.
Syair is a type of poetry from Malaysia that has four lines with an AAAA rhyme scheme. These poems are meant to be performed and chanted in front of a crowd and often during historical or mythical events.
Example:

Thầy's essence perseveres
because of his peace we release our fears
meditating with intention we are sincere
grateful for his legacy in us as our mirror

- Lindsey Leong, aka HELLA famous

It's time to reset and restart.

Prompt #1:
Reflect on these questions:
What is your source of life? What does it look like? Feel like? Sound like? In what areas of your life do you feel you are pushing too hard? In which areas of your life would you like to see more flow?

Prompt #2:
Write or draw from a place of courage and authenticity and do not worry about being perfect.
What do you want to bring to fruition in the near future?
What are your hopes and aspirations?

Prompt #3:
List five dreams you have for today and for the future.

Self-care Tips

- Get a massage to help relieve you from tense or sore muscles, body pain, stress, anxiety, and depression.
- Get enough sleep because your body and brain need it!
- Get active and dance to your favorite song.

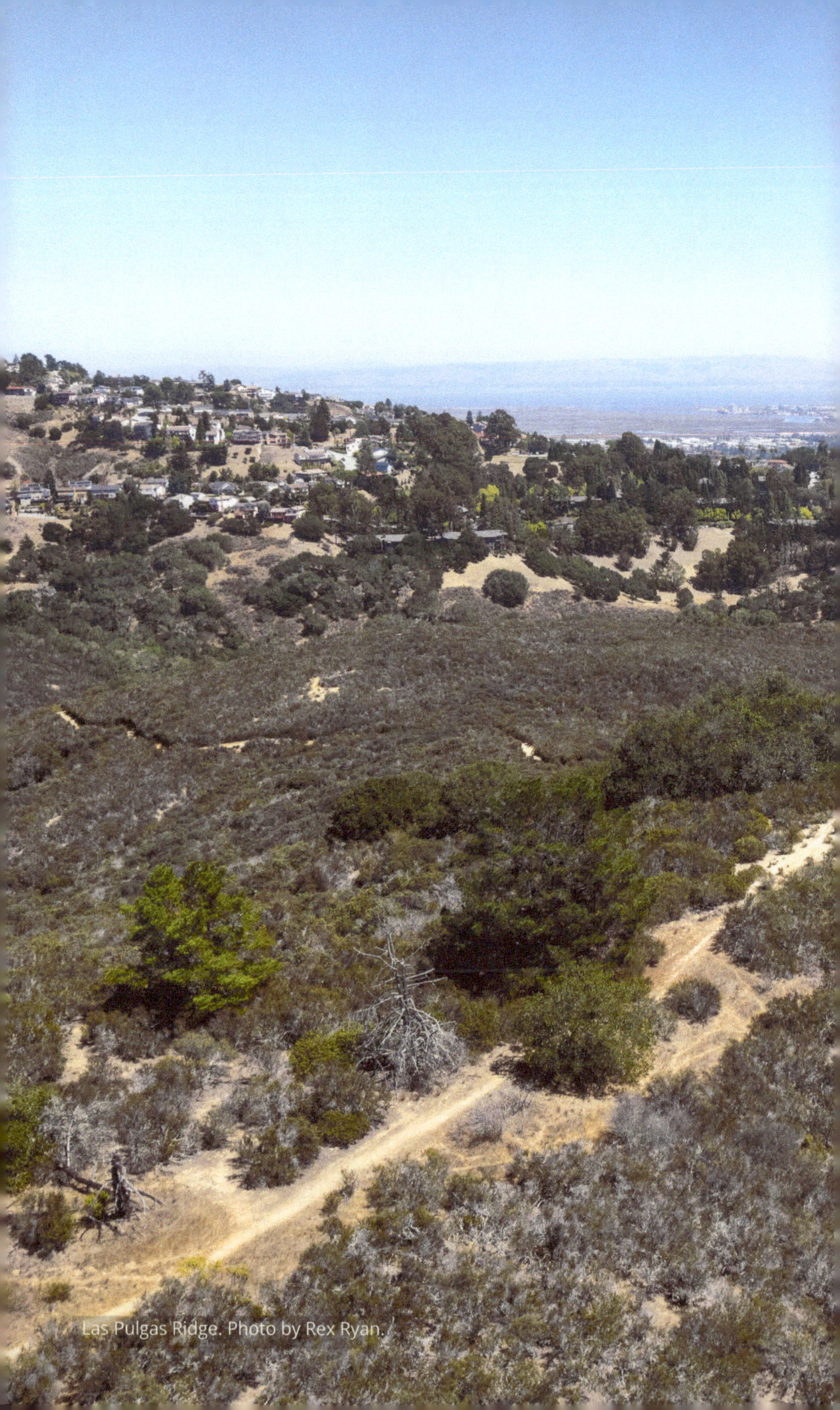
Las Pulgas Ridge. Photo by Rex Ryan.

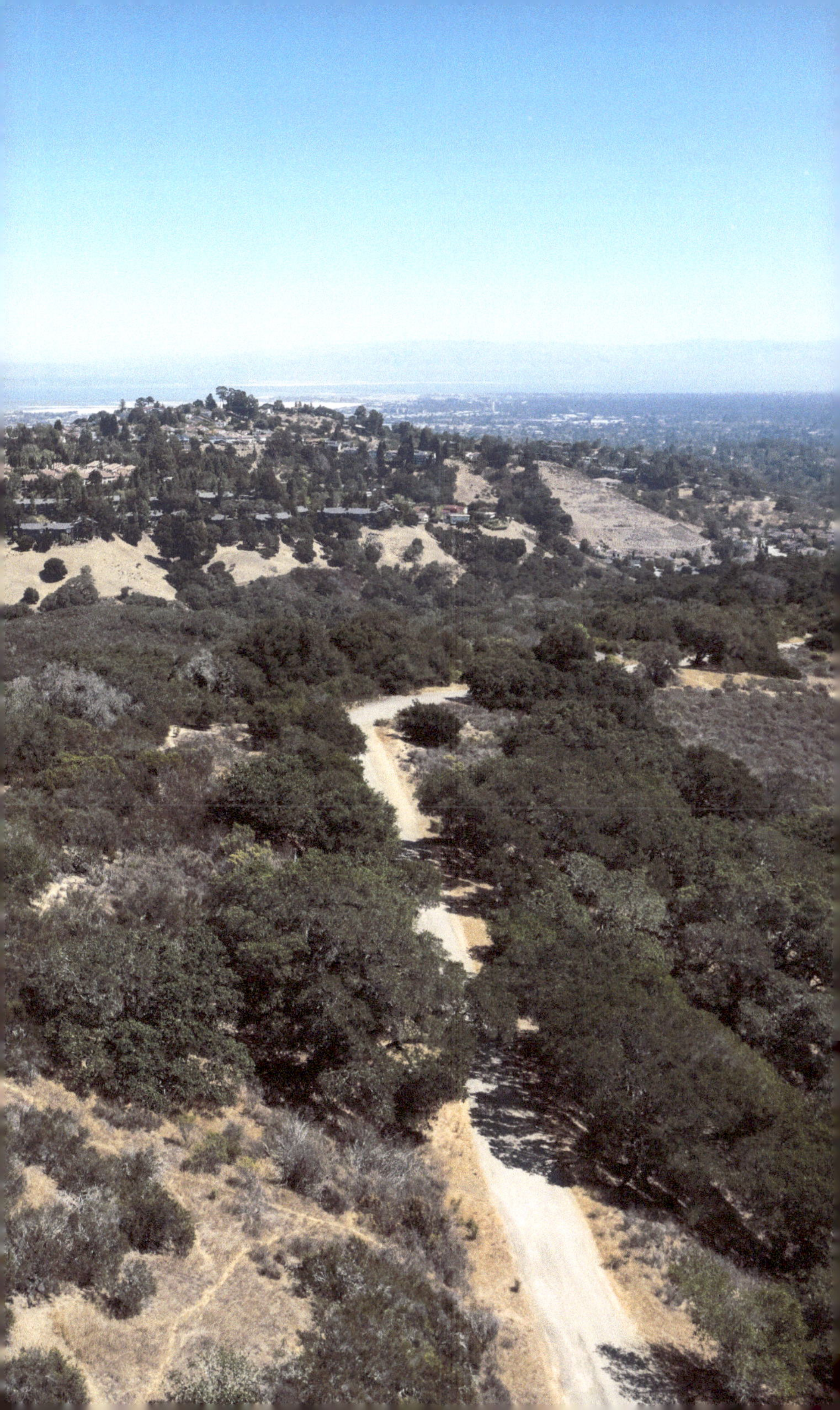

Mother Earth
Poem by Kristina Robertson

I slowly drift out into the Red Lotus Sea,
petals propagated by reflective uncertainties.
Stirring my limbs feverishly,
I feel as if I am drowning.
A hallowed seashell,
silenced from the rolling waves.
Find me running barefoot in the forest,
grounded to the dirt,
hair blowing crossly in the wind.
I stumble on the branches and fall into Mother Earth.
Her vibration shudders the tips of my fingers,
I lay like I was 2:50 on a clock,
stretching every muscle while emerging from nature's womb.
This American soil is my sanctuary.
I am like a dandelion blowing in a hurricane,
wishing to feel poised in my own mixed freckled skin.
I smell the moss and wet tree trunks,
purest air to breathe.
I breathe it all in and out,
And fall back into the sea of empathy haloing my body,
riding the waves of my emotions.
I tread softly,
reflect underneath the surface of my confusion.
Floating to allow the salt to heal my apprehension.
Remembering that I am never alone in this world
when I have Mother and her roots inside.

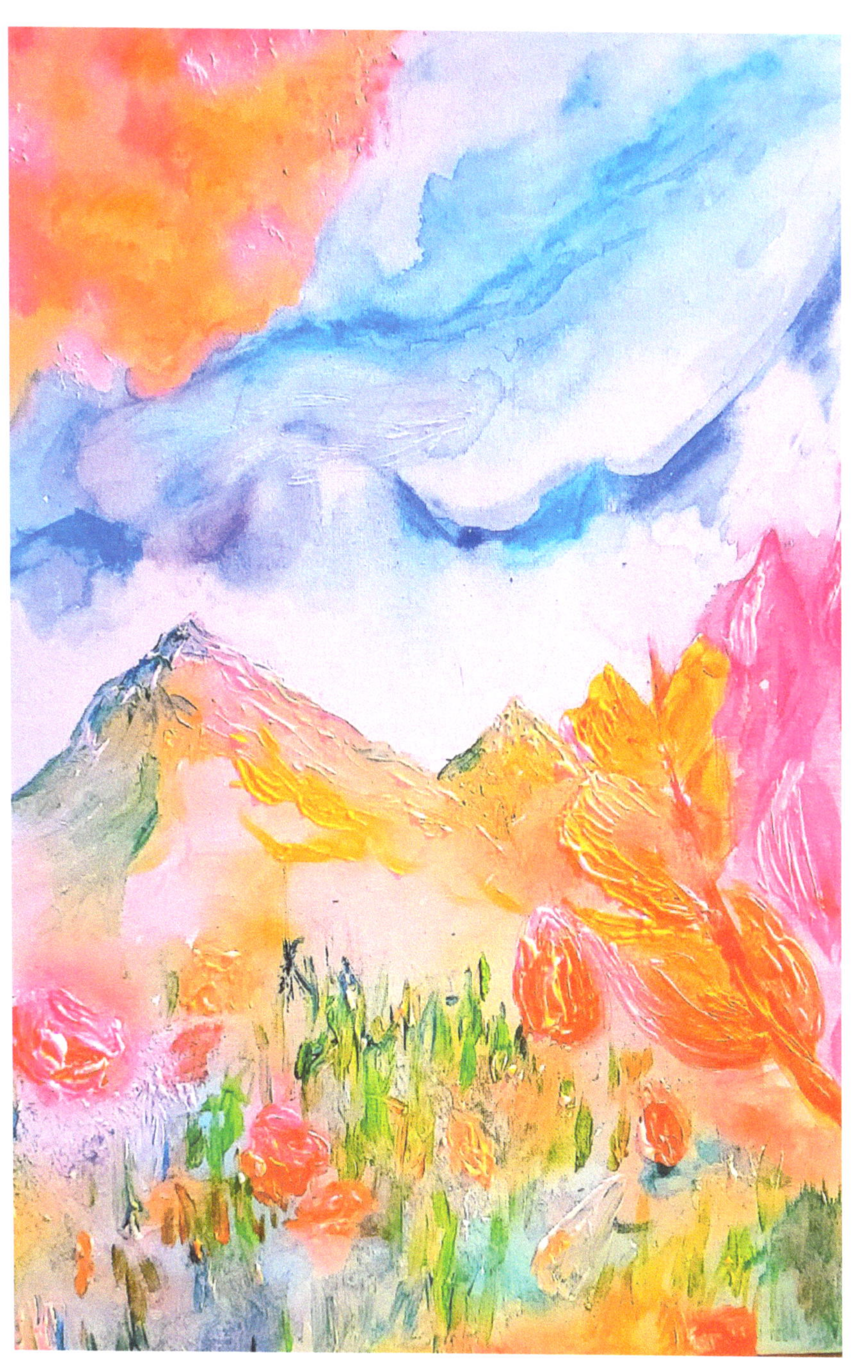

Samantha Tran (age 13), *Bloom in Color*, watercolor and acrylic, 2022

Walk #5

BORN TO BE WILD

Ikigai is the Japanese concept of finding purpose and value in this life and how this ideology can help you find the path to happiness. Having a sense of direction can help you live a more fulfilled life. Take the time to re-evaluate our values to see if we embody these values in our daily lives. It can be as simple as engaging in your favorite hobby or activity to helping others to uncover your life's higher purpose or calling.

Spend time contemplating your path and life's purpose and joy.

Meditation from Plum Village App

Select: Meditations > Guided Meditations > Short Meditations
Gratitude for the Four Elements by Brother Phap Dung (5:40 mins)

Select: Meditations > Guided Meditations > Touching the Earth
Guided Deep Relaxation and Gratitude for Our Body by Sister Chan Khong (11:36 mins)

Select: Silent Meditations
Silent meditations to try when you are ready to hear your inner voice better. Start with short ones and work your way up to longer ones.

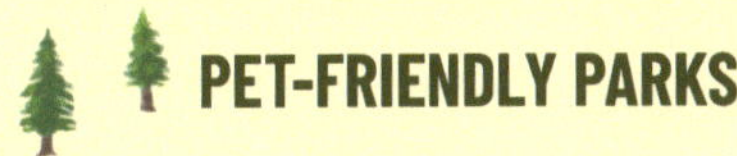

PET-FRIENDLY PARKS

Calero County Park via Rancho San Vicente 
21151 McKean Rd, San Jose, CA 95120

There is a great diversity of terrain in this park. The trails offer you and your pets an excellent workout with spectacular views, or you can choose a shorter walk with less climbing for a quick half-day spent outdoors.

For a nice out-and-back hike to *Lisa's Lookout* (2.7 miles one-way), park at the Rancho San Vicente entrance of Calero County Park off of McKean Boulevard to enjoy verdant views of the Almaden Hills and pack a snack to enjoy at *Lisa's Lookout*. Watch for grazing cattle, which is a regular occurrence on this trail.

If you choose to continue past the vista point on *Lisa Killough trail*, turn left towards Calero Reservoir onto *Cottle trail* for a loop that includes groves of fragrant bay laurel and views of the Calero Reservoir (8 miles total, including the 2.7 miles to *Lisa's Lookout*).

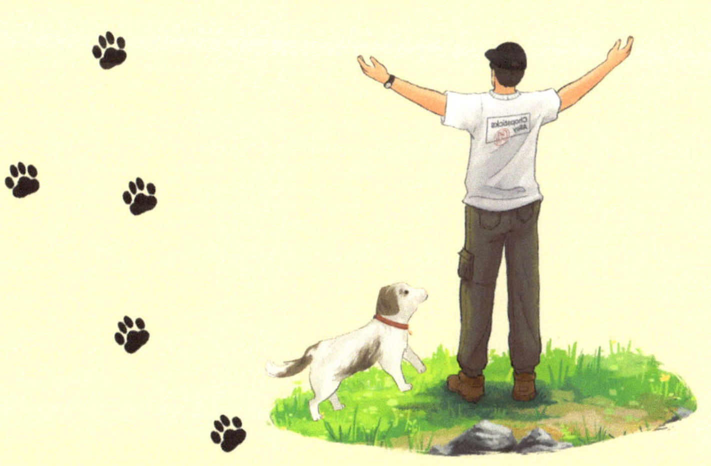

Pulgas Ridge Open Space Preserve
167 Edmonds Rd, Redwood City, CA 94062

This preserve has a 17.5-acre off-leash area for dogs. You can access it by *Hassler Loop* and *Blue Oak Trail*. Dogs must be under voice control; owners must have a leash on hand and pack out all waste. In other areas of the preserve, dogs must be leashed.

All trails of this preserve allow dogs, so don't feel you can only explore the off-leash area. The *Dusky-Footed Woodrat Trail* will take you to the ridgeline for spectacular views.

Take *Blue Oak* to *Hassler Trail* (make sure not to stay on *Hassler Loop*), which connects to the *Woodrat Trail*.

The preserve is popular on weekends, so get there early for the best parking. As with any hike, remember to check your dog for ticks afterward–especially behind the ears, neck, and chest area.

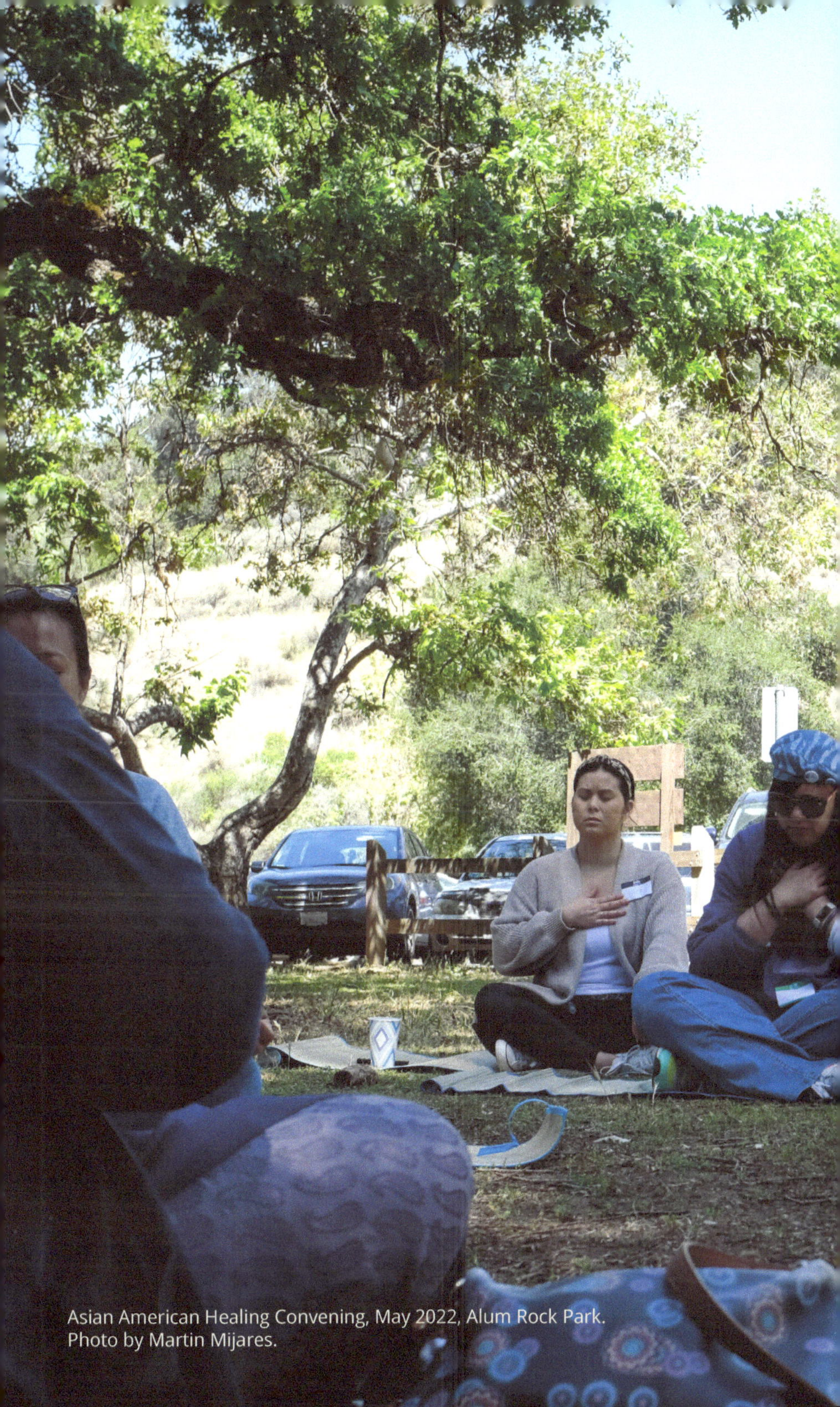

Asian American Healing Convening, May 2022, Alum Rock Park.
Photo by Martin Mijares.

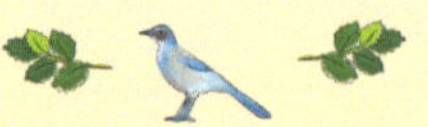

Write a poem following Pantum's poetry tradition.
Pantum is a poetic style from Indonesia that follows an ABAB rhyme scheme. The first two lines are traditionally a proverb or riddle, while the second two lines are the answer and meaning.
Example:

Leaves fall with a changing season
does change activate the self compassion of being brave
wood, fire, earth, metal, water are our reason
create, release, renew, reflect healing is a constant wave

- Lindsey Leong, aka HELLA famous

Uncover your purpose.

Prompt #1:
Reflect on your life:
Do you know your life's purpose yet?
What actions align with your values?
What brings you joy and comes with ease in your life?
Whom can you trust to be part of this journey with you?

Prompt #2:

In the present tense, write or draw a short story about how you've been able to live the life that you want to have.
Who and what resources can help you get there?
What steps are you taking?
How do you feel about your story?
Rewrite your story until you fall in love with it!

Prompt #3:

List five actions that you can take in this phase of your life.
Which one excites you the most?
How are you committing them to your schedule?

Self-care Tips

- Surround yourself with happy people with a positive outlook on life or those with the same hobby as you.
- Think of someone who has been there for you and write them a thank you note to show gratitude.
- Give back by donating or volunteering in your community or for a park.
- Seek professional help, such as speaking to a counselor or joining a support group.

Calligraphy Brush
Poem by Brandon Luu

I've only ever seen it held
Carefully, lightly
Like a bird, perched
Upon a slender branch

And then, as if holding a breath
The brush moves forward
With deliberate slowness
With steady purpose:

Contemplate
The nature of green earth
Of gentle rain
And patient stone

Consider the animal
That comes to rest
After a lifetime
Of wandering

Allow yourself time
To forgive and let go
The way leaves must fall
The way day must end

The cricket leaps
As does the frog
Into the moon
And pond

The brush is set down
The work now done
And the letter appears
Like a silent prayer

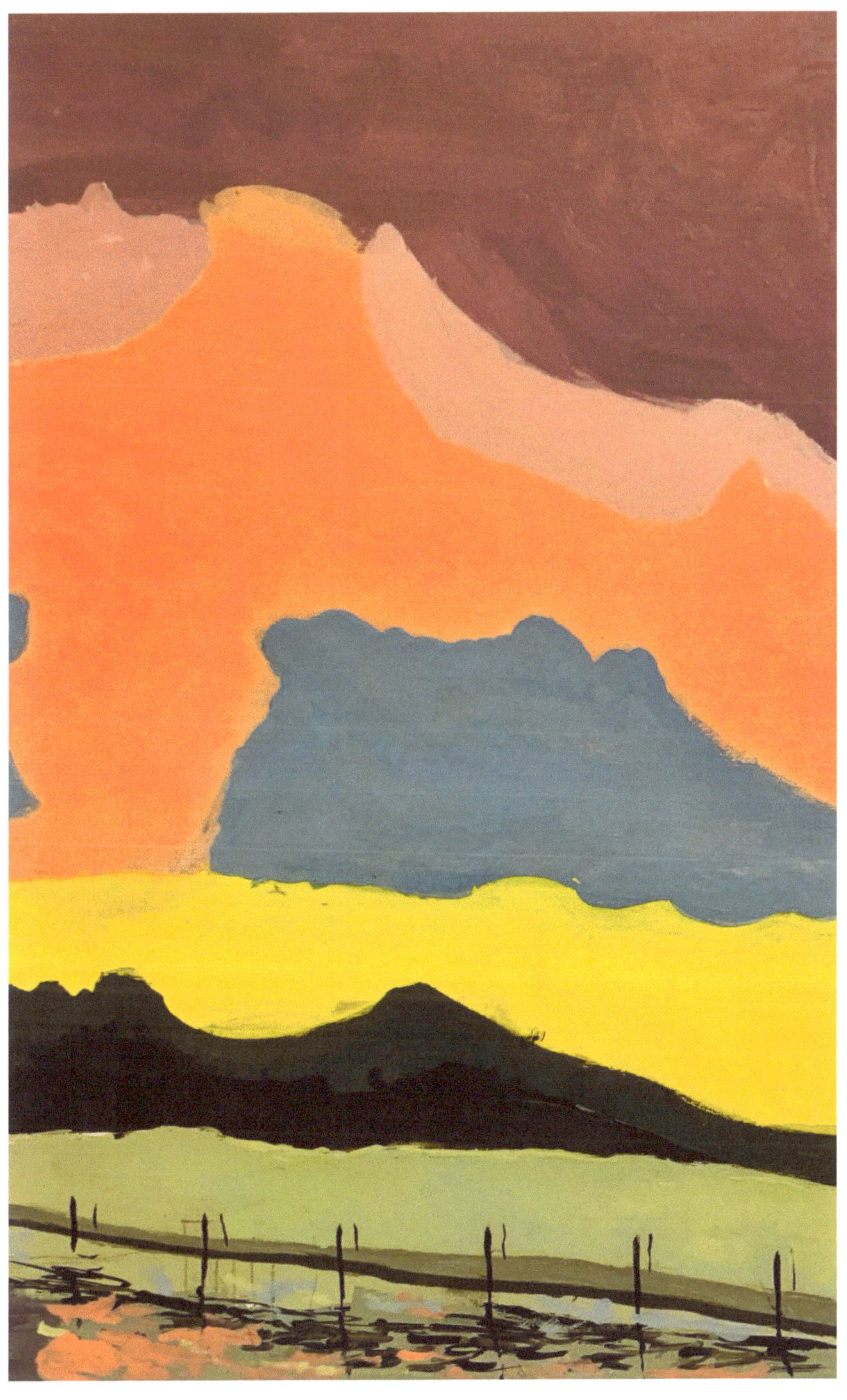

Luke Ma (age 6), *Sunset over a lake*, acrylic on canvas, 2022

Silicon Valley Vista Point. Photo by Rex Ryan.

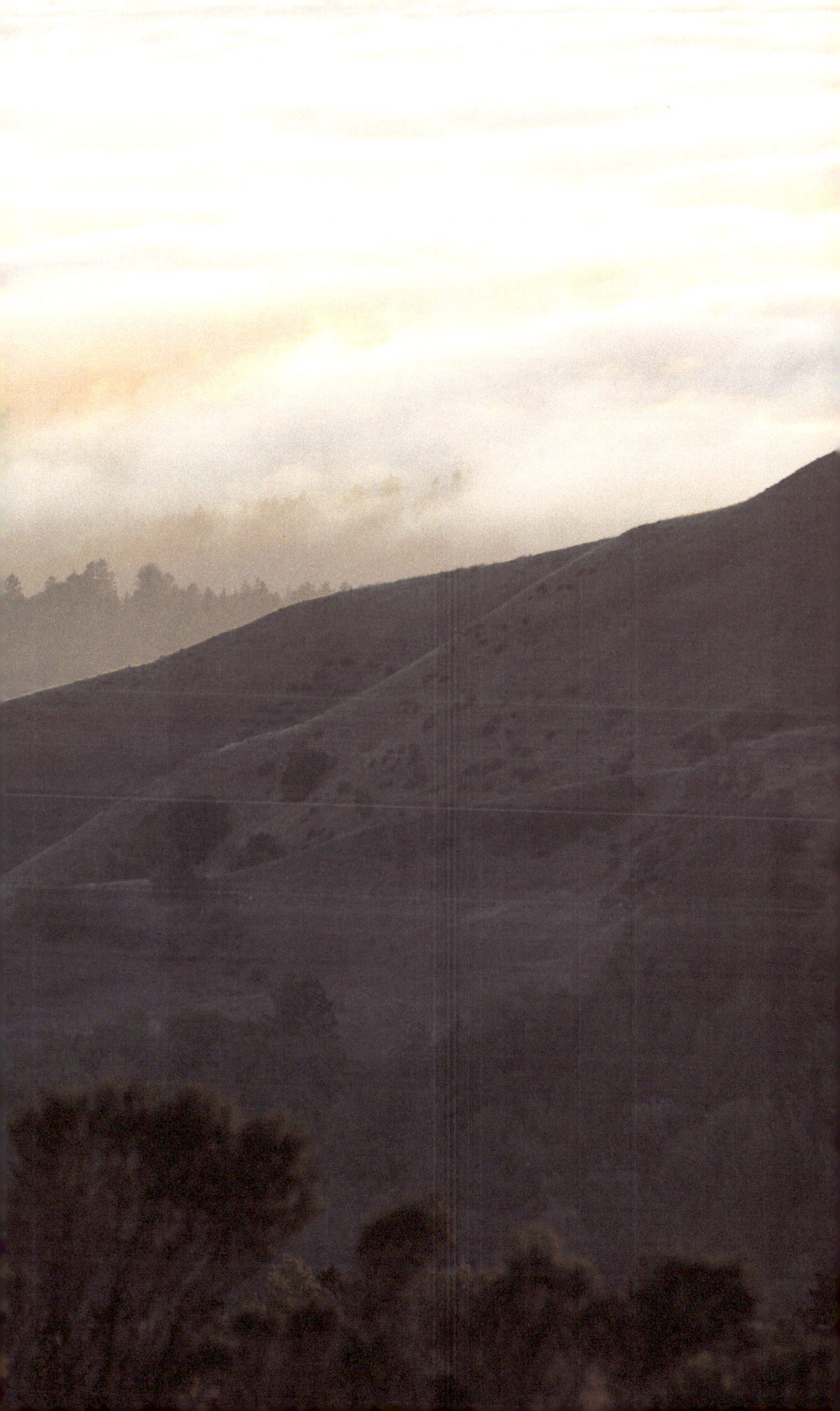

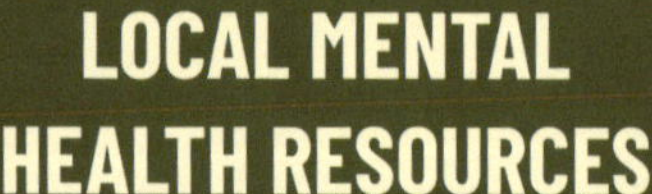

LOCAL MENTAL HEALTH RESOURCES

Behavioral Health Services - County of Santa Clara
The Behavioral Health Call Center is the entry point for access to all Santa Clara County behavioral health services. The center provides support for individuals and families who are in crisis; considering suicide; or struggling with mental illness, substance use, or both.

Anyone seeking help or support can dial these phone numbers to inquire about services. Language assistance services are available free of charge.

Mental Health and Substance Use Services
Phone number: 1 (800) 704 - 0900
(TTY: 800-855-7100 or 711)

Crisis and Suicide Prevention Lifeline 24/7
Phone number: 1 (800) 704 - 0900, press 1
Dial 988 for local 408, 650 and 669 area codes
Text RENEW to 741741

Asian Americans for Community Involvement (AACI)
Learn about a collaborative approach to whole-person care.

2400 Moorpark Ave., Ste 300, San Jose, CA 95128
Phone number: (408) 975 – 2730

Vietnamese American Service Center (VASC)
County of Santa Clara
VASC provides health and wellness workshops and activities.

2410 Senter Rd., 2nd Floor, San Jose, CA 95111
Phone number: (408) 518 – 6200

National Alliance on Mental Illness (NAMI) Santa Clara County
1150 S. Bascom Ave., Suite 24, San Jose, CA 95128

If you or someone you know struggles with mental illness, call: NAMI-SCC HELPLINE
Phone number: (408) 453 – 0400 x1
Office Hours: Monday - Friday, 10:00am – 6:00pm
Walk-in Hours: Monday - Friday, 10:00am – 2:00pm

For after hours support, leave a voicemail at (408) 453 - 0400 x4
Monday - Friday, 6:00pm - 9:00pm
Saturday and Sunday, 12:00pm - 6:00pm

LOCAL ORGANIZATIONS & RESOURCES

Veggielution
The mission of Veggielution is to connect people from diverse backgrounds outdoors through food and farming to build community in East San José.

Emma Prusch Farm Park
647 S King Rd., San Jose, CA, 95116
(408) 753-6705
veggielution.org
info@veggielution.org
Volunteer Opportunities

Guadalupe River Park Conservancy
Do something good for the environment by helping to maintain parks and gardens.

438 Coleman Ave., San Jose, CA 95110
grpg.org
Volunteer Opportunities

Parks, Recreation, and Neighborhood Services (PRNS) City of San José
They have volunteer opportunities at local parks and gardens in San Jose, such as the Municipal Rose Garden, Japanese Friendship Garden, and Alum Rock Park.

sanjoseca.gov
ParkVolunteer@sanjoseca.gov
Volunteer Opportunities

Keep Coyote Creek Beautiful
They have volunteer opportunities to help restore Coyote Creek through cleanups.

5339 Prospect Rd. #281, San Jose, CA 95129
(408) 372-7053
www.keepcoyotecreekbeautiful.org
deb@keepcoyotecreekbeautiful.org

ANIMAL & PET RESCUES

All Animal Rescue and Friends (AARF)
This all-volunteer rescue organization focuses on reuniting lost & found animals within our community.

PO Box 941
San Martin, CA 94046
aarflove.org
Volunteer Opportunities

Dogwood Animal Rescue
This organization supports animals and the people who love them through rescue services, rehoming, spay & neuter, and education.

1415 Fulton Rd.
Suite 205, Box 432,
Santa Rosa, CA 95403
dogwoodanimalrescue.org
Volunteer Opportunities

***Note:** websites and contact information may have changed since the completion of this guide.

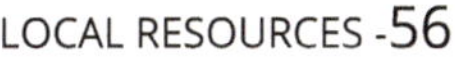

CONTRIBUTORS

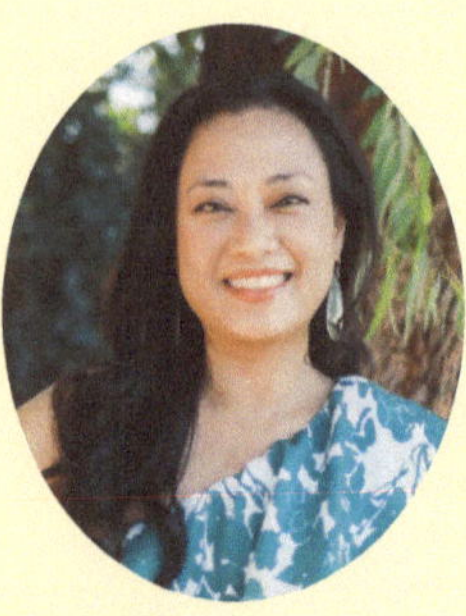

Trami Cron
Creative Director, Writer, Editor

Trami is the founder and Executive Artistic Director of Chopsticks Alley Art and Chopsticks Alley, an online publication. She is a cultural organizer, producer, and host of talk shows and podcasts. Trami is the author of *VietnamEazy*, a novel about mother-daughter relationships, and the creative director and co-author of *ARTventure Down the Mekong*, an art-making book based on Southeast Asian arts and cultures. She has a BA in Marketing from the University of Utah.

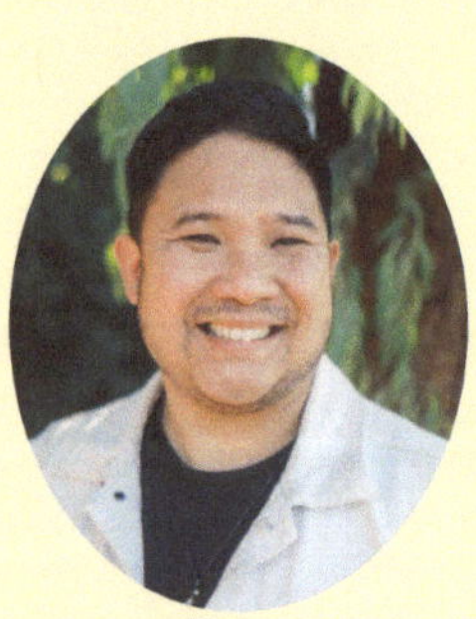

Anthony Lê
Writing Prompts, Photographer

Anthony's journey embodies the remarkable potential of transformation, from breaking free of tech illusions to embracing his mission of nurturing lives and deepening human connections. He is a life and leadership guide to empower individuals and communities for meaningful change. He has been a Deputy Director of the Asian Pacific American Leadership Institute, a Vietnamese-American Roundtable, and EM Collective board member, and a facilitator for many leadership programs nationwide. He is also a photographer who has leveraged this art medium to connect deeper to his mindfulness practice and the people around him.

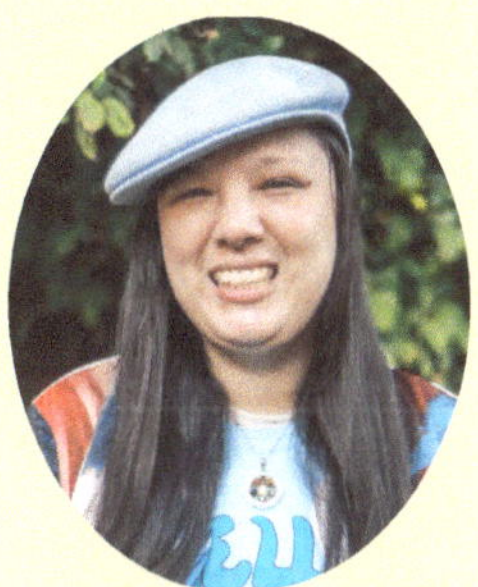

Lindsey Leong
Poetry Prompts

Lindsey, aka HELLA famous, is a third-generation Chinese American spoken word artist, host, curator, and community organizer with over twenty years of experience. Her Spoken Word EP *I Am A Metaphor* is currently streaming on all platforms. Lindsey was recently named one of the fifty-six activists selected to participate in East Bay Meditation Center's year-long *Practice In Trans-formative Action* program.

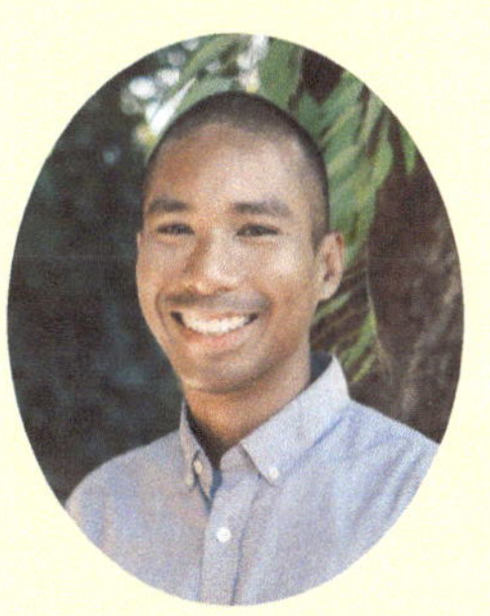

Jerome Ilagan
Park Locations

Jerome is a former Community Engagement Intern at Peninsula Open Space Trust (POST). He contributed to POST's large-scale community events supporting DEI initiatives, including Dr. Robin Wall Kimmerer's lectures, the *Representation Matters FilmFestival*, and MidPen's *50th Anniversary Coastside Community* celebration.

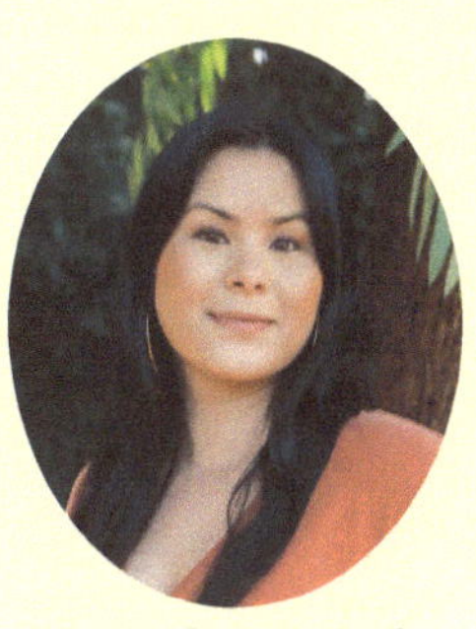

Saysolina Sath
Mental Health Tips

Saysolina is a mental health educator and advocate. She focuses on community engagement and outreach to spread awareness, provide resources, and help stop mental health stigma, especially within the Asian American and Pacific Islander Communities. She has a BA in Psychology, a Minor in Child Development, and an MA in Counselor Education from San Jose State University.

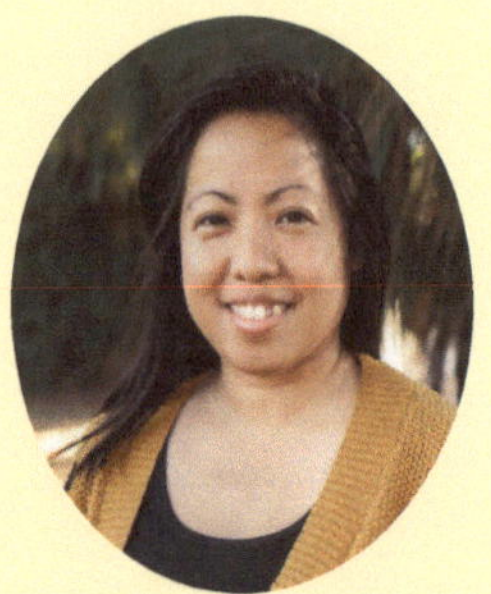

Roan Victor
Illustrator

Roan is a Filipino-American fine art painter and muralist. Co-founder and operator for 11 years of the now defunct The Arsenal SJ, she is currently part of a collective of artists with a shared space called Know Future Gallery, based in Japantown San Jose. Lush foliage of California native flora and fauna are common themes in Roan's artworks, and her digital illustrations can be found throughout this guide book.

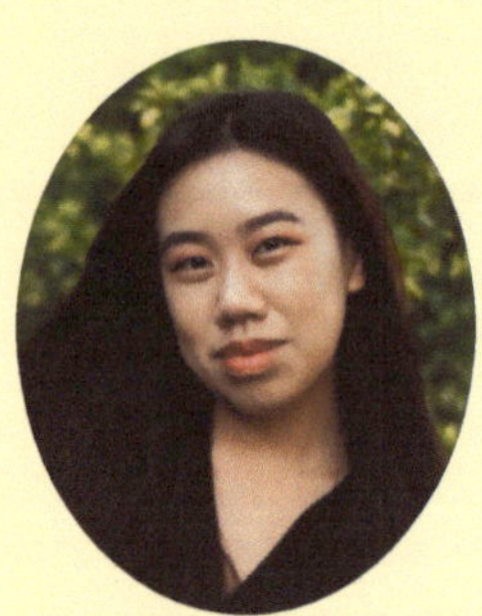

Elaine Li
Illustrator

Elaine is a San Jose State University Animation & Illustration Program graduate with a BFA. As a visual developement artist and 3D modeler, she enjoys designing characters and environments in 2D or 3D. She has worked on various projects, from animated short films to video games.

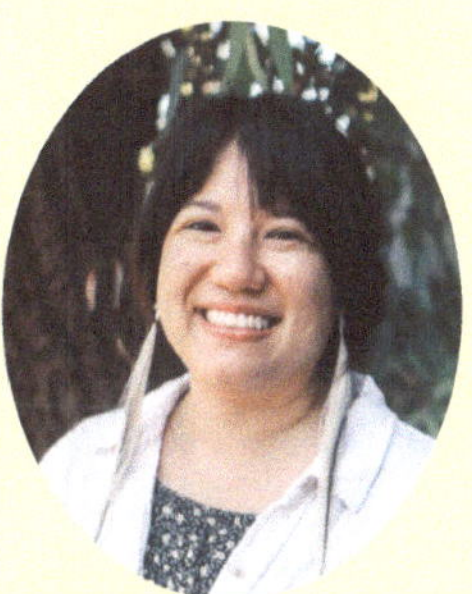

Cynthia Cao
Book Designer

Cynthia is a Vietnamese-American visual artist primarily working with printmaking, painting, and photography. She has worked as the Exhibition Designer for Chopsticks Alley Art since 2018. She earned her BFA in Pictorial Arts with a Minor in Art History and Visual Culture from San Jose State University. Cynthia enjoys horseback riding, hiking in the backcountry, and gardening in her free time.

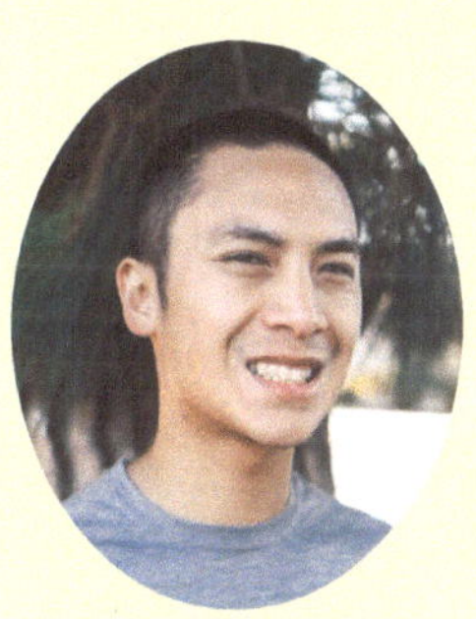

Rex Ryan
Photographer

Rex is a Filipino-American entrepreneur. His three passions are entrepreneurship, real estate, and the outdoors. He is currently the co-founder of ACRE New Mexico in Albuquerque. Rex hopes to inspire more people to follow their creative passions and to take the road less taken.

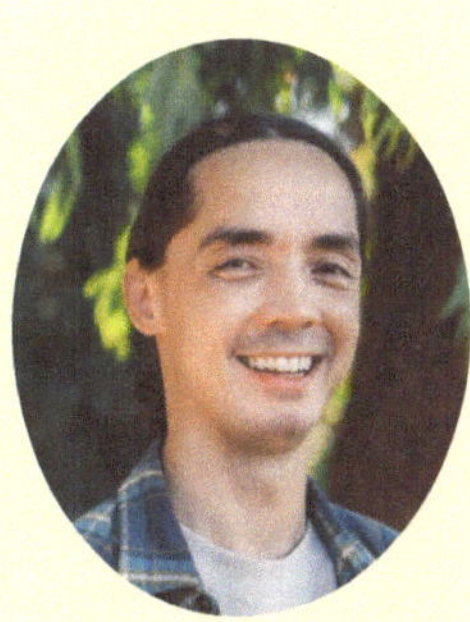

Martin Mijares
Photographer

Martin is a designer making technology user-friendly. When not behind a desk, he actively participates in the art community (also food community). He enjoys working behind the scenes to create and shine a light on human experiences. He uses his creative toolkit to capture Chopsticks Alley's programs and events into moments everyone can enjoy.

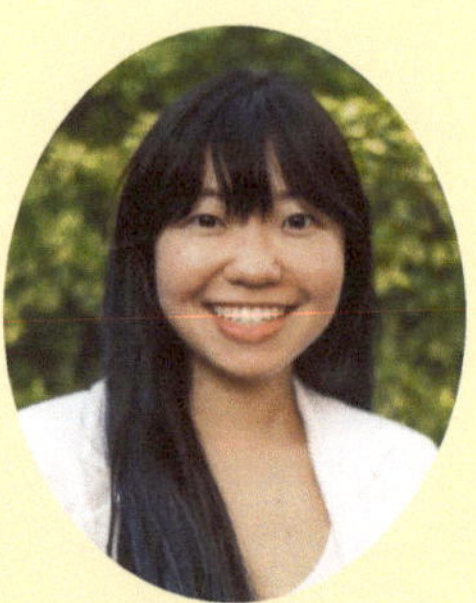

Esther Young
Copyeditor

Esther has written for Bay Area publications such as Content Magazine and Metro Silicon Valley since 2018. During the day, she works as the community engagement specialist for the School of Arts and Culture at the Mexican Heritage Plaza – a role she leverages to connect and uplift San Jose's rich creative communities.
A singer-songwriter at heart, she is active in the local music scene and currently co-hosts Chopsticks Alley Art's monthly open mic showcase.

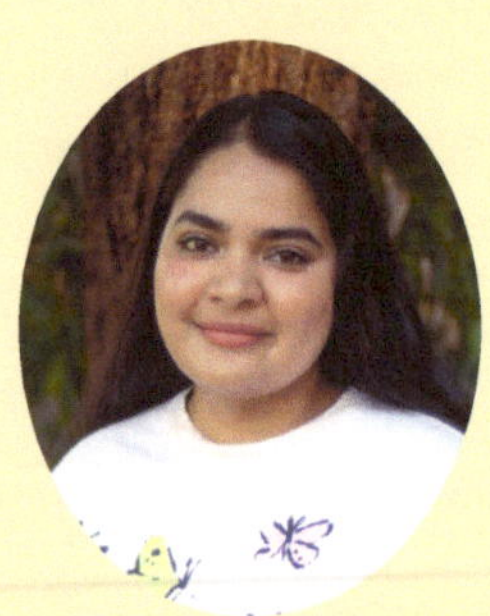

Harleen Kaur
Copyeditor

Harleen is a current student at UCLA finishing up her BA in Philosophy. She worked on Chopsticks Alley's first book *ARTventure Down the Mekong*.

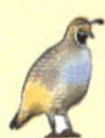

ARTISTS & POETS

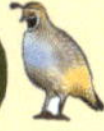

XXII **Lindsey Leong, aka HELLA famous,**
"And So It Is"
hellafamous.com
instagram: @hellafamous11

XXIII **Phillip Hua**
Deciduous Deal, UV cured acrylic print on acrylic with gold metal leafed panel, 2019
philliphua.com

3 **Marisa Lin**, "In Our Name"
instagram: @marisawrites

4 **Cynthia Cao**
Mt Umunhum #4, watercolor on paper, 2018
cynthiacao.com
instagram: @hownowbrowncao_

5 **Julie Dang**
Quỳnh + Tiên, digital illustration, 2022
instagram: @islandofdang

13 **Rey Simpauco**
Breathe, digital illustration, 2022
reysimpauco.com
instagram: @reysimpauco

14 **Yan Yin Choy,** "Laundry and Taxes"
yanyinchoy.com
instagram: @yanyinchoy

23 **Hang Huynh**, "Memories"

23 **Hang Huynh**, *In my memory,* digital photo collage, 2023

24 **Hang Huynh**, *New beginning*, digital photo collage, 2023
hanghuynh.com
instagram: @hahu.sj.sg

31

Louisa Zhao
Misty Morning in the Bay, watercolor, 2022
facebook.com/artassoul

32

Brian Le, "Epistula Heroidi (Letter to a Heroine)"
windswaves.wordpress.com

41

Kristina Robertson, "Mother Earth"
instagram: @kristina_robertson18

42

Samantha Tran (age 13)
Bloom in Color, watercolor and acrylic, 2022
instagram: @samanthatran.08

49

Brandon Luu, "Calligraphy Brush"
instagram: @bluubasaur

50

Luke Ma (age 6)
Sunset over a Lake, acrylic on canvas, 2022
email: Louisa Zhao (Luke's mother)
louisa786@hotmail.com

ACKNOWLEDGEMENTS

We would like to thank all past and present AAH organizers, Medi-Veggie team, graphics designers, and artists for inspiring and providing content for this guide:

Eric Bui, Coby Chuang, Trami Cron, Smita Garg, Ed.D,
Mina Mehta Gates, Ashley Hin, Hang Huynh, Anthony Lê,
Lindsey Leong, Martin Mijares, Matthew Molcillo,
Vinh G. Nguyen, Saysalina Sath, and Esther Young.

Community Partners and Sponsors:

CATS (Contemporary Arts Theatre Scene)
Joanne Ho
Leianne Lamb

POST (Peninsula Open Space Trust)
Jerome Ilagan
Mark Medeiros
Megan Nguyen

VALLEY WATER
Tiffany Chao
Kristen Yasukawa

This guide book was made possible by a grant from the San Jose Office of Racial Equity, sponsorship from POST, and is funded in part by the California Arts Council, a state agency.

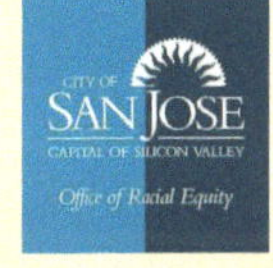

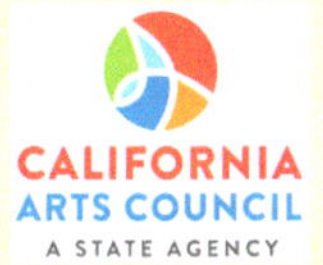

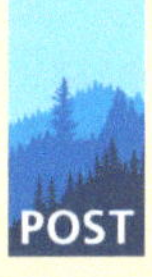

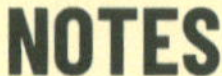

NOTES

Poetry Traditions

"Types of Asian and Pacific Poetry." RSS, poetryteatime.com/blog/types-of-asian-and-pacific-poetry.

Taoist Traditions

"Cultural Associations of Water in Early Chinese and Indian Religion and Medicine." Association for Asian Studies, 5 July 2023, www.asianstudies.org/publications/eaa/archives/cultural-associations-of-water-in-early-chinese-and-indian-religion-and-medicine/.

Parks Recommendations

"Castle Rock Hiking: Saratoga Gap Trail and Ridge Trail." Castle Rock Hiking: Saratoga Gap Trail and Ridge Trail, trailingahead.blogspot.com/2019/07/castle-rock-hiking-saratoga-gap-trail.html.

Meier, Eve. "Calero Creek Trail (Fall/Winter)." Santa Clara Valley Audubon Society, Santa Clara Valley Audubon Society, 8 Dec. 2022, scvas.org/self-guided-birding/calero-creek-trail-in-fallwinter.

Ikigai Traditions

Dayman, Lucy. "Ikigai: The Japanese Concept of Finding Purpose in Life." Savvy Tokyo, 24 Oct. 2022, savvytokyo.com/ikigai-japanese-concept-finding-purpose-life/.

Nature Healing

Mani, Mukesh. "54 Profound Quotes on the Healing Power of Nature." OutofStress.Com, Outofstress.com, 6 Mar. 2020, www.outofstress.com/healing-power-of-nature-quotes/.

"Changes in Recreational Behaviors of Outdoor Enthusiasts during the COVID-19 Pandemic: Analysis across Urban and Rural Communities." Academic.Oup.Com, academic.oup.com/jue/article/6/1/juaa020/5892687.

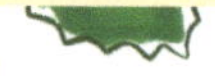

Travel, Love, and Taste of Thailand. "Songkran: The Value behind Thai New Year and Water Festival." Taste of Thailand, 17 Apr. 2019, tasteofthailand.org/songkran-the-value-behind-thai-new-year-and-water-festival/.

Cambodia Proverbs
"Cambodian Proverbs in English Quotes and Sayings." Cambodian Proverbs in English and Sayings, www.quotes.oneindiaonline.com/cambodian-proverbs-in-english.php.

Vietnamese Proverbs
Slife. "Vietnamese Proverbs (Tục Ngữ Việt Nam)." The Spiritual Life, 26 Sept. 2021, slife.org/vietnamese-proverbs/.

Malaysian Proverbs
"Malay Proverbs on Nature Archives." Famous Inspirational Proverbs, Quotes, Sayings, www.inspirationalstories.com/proverbs/t/malay-on-nature/.

Studies about Public Parks
Madalinsky, Jim. "Public Parks Seeing Surge in Attendance during Pandemic." WTAE, WTAE, 4 Sept. 2020, www.wtae.com/article/public-parks-seeing-surge-during-pandemic/33929115.

Mental Health Tips
"Better Information. Better Health." WebMD, WebMD, www.webmd.com/.

"What Is Psychological Wholeness? Are You There Yet?" Promises Behavioral Health, 14 July 2013, www.promises.com/addiction-blog/what-is-psychological-wholeness-are-you-there-yet/.

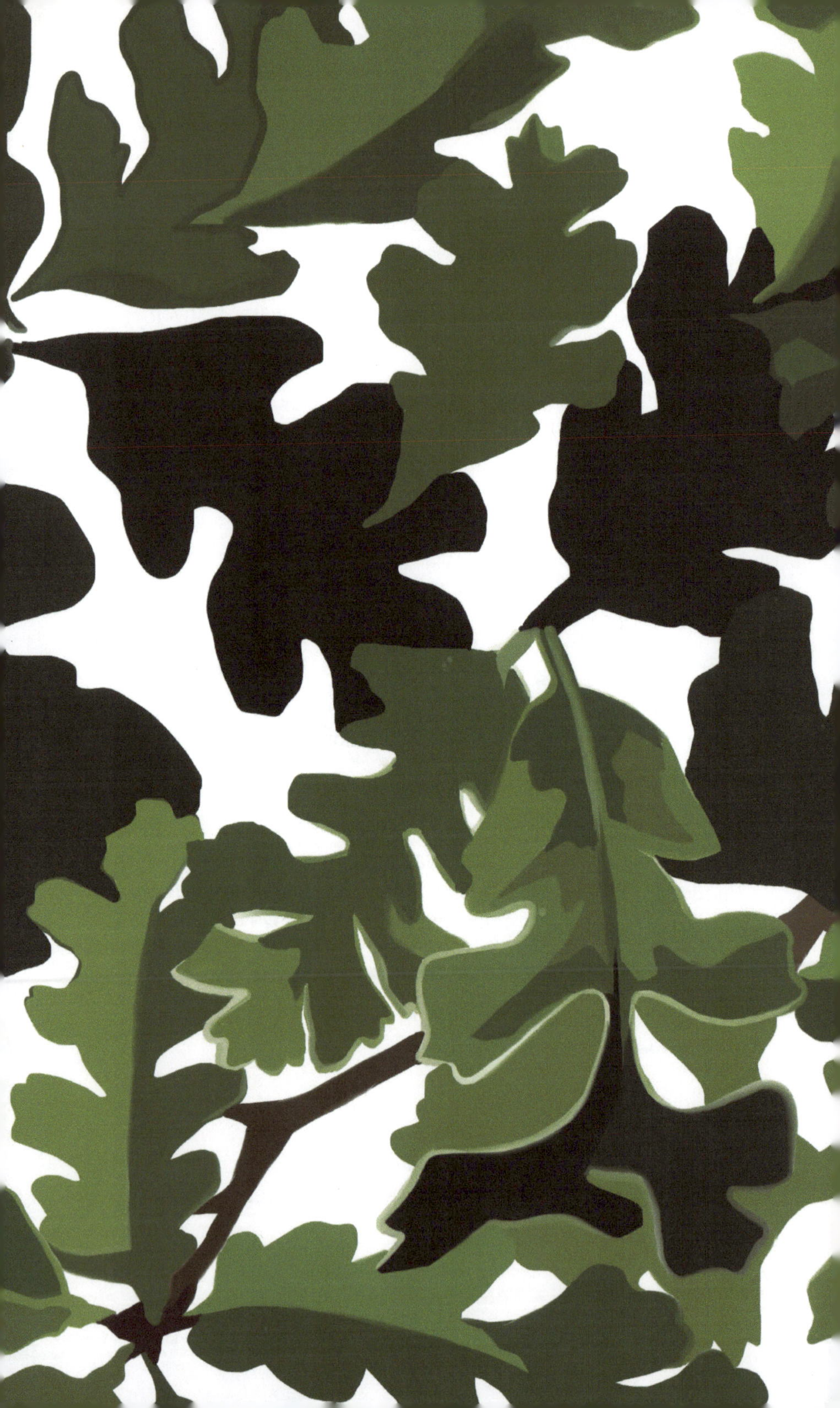

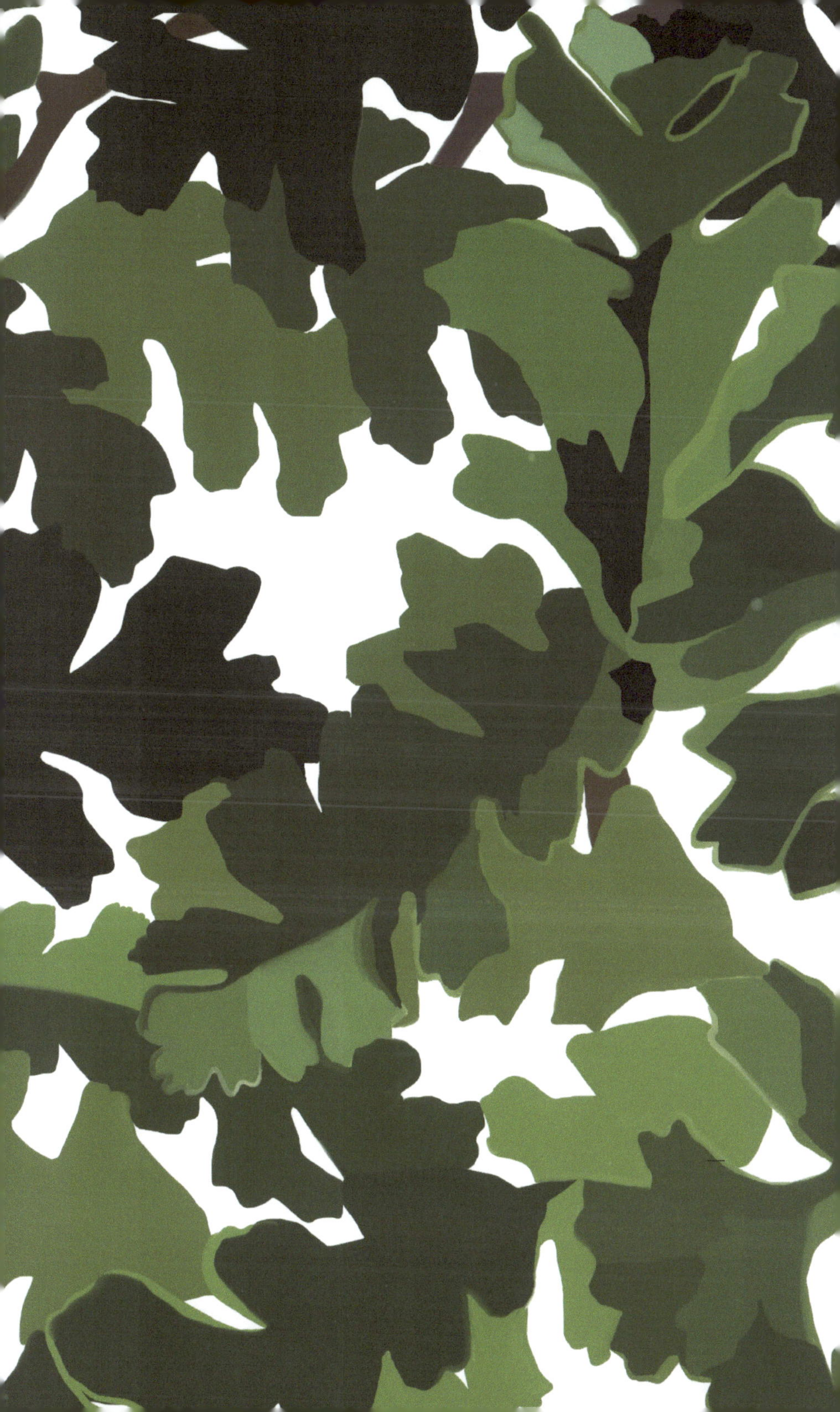

www.ingramcontent.com/pod-product-compliance
Lightning Source LLC
LaVergne TN
LVHW052307100826
845147LV00006B/697

* 9 7 9 8 2 1 8 3 7 7 1 8 2 *